BECOMING AWARE OF
THE BIG-YOU

EVER ASKED YOURSELF WHAT IS MY TRUE PURPOSE?
CHANGE YOUR CHANNEL
YOUR IDEAL FUTURE IS JUST A CLICK AWAY

By

Madge and John Morgan

MAPLE PUBLISHERS

Becoming Aware of THE BIG-YOU

Author: Madge and John Morgan

Copyright © Madge and John Morgan (2024)

The right of Madge and John Morgan to be identified as author of this work has been asserted by the author in accordance with section 77 and 78 of the Copyright, Designs and Patents Act 1988.

First Published in 2024

ISBN 978-1-83538-308-7 (Paperback)
978-1-83538-309-4 (E-Book)

Cover Design and Book Layout by:
White Magic Studios
www.whitemagicstudios.co.uk

Published by:
Maple Publishers
Fairbourne Drive, Atterbury,
Milton Keynes,
MK10 9RG, UK
www.maplepublishers.com

A CIP catalogue record for this title is available from the British Library.

All rights reserved. No part of this book may be reproduced or translated by any form or by any means, electronic or mechanical, including photocopying, recording or by any information storage and retrieval system without written permission from the author.

The book is a work of fiction. Unless otherwise indicated, all the names, characters, places and incidents are either the product of the author's imagination or used in a fictitious manner. Any resemblance to actual people living or dead, events or locales is entirely coincidental, and the Publisher hereby disclaims any responsibility for them.

Further Information and Contacting the author:

If you wish to correspond with Madge and John about their work, courses, workshops and speaking engagements. Please write to them at the following address:

Email:- How@morganccs.com
Website:- www.MorganCCS.com

CONTENTS

Glossary 5

Context 9

The Author's Story 12

My Awakening to Awareness 15

How to Use This Book 20

Chapter 1: The Human Life Experience (HLE) Model 21

Chapter 2: The 3.5.1. Method 23

Chapter 3: The Lucky Formula 43

Chapter 4: The Two Realms: Topics on Awareness 57

Chapter 5: The Trapped Earth—Concluding Thoughts 196

Chapter 6: Epilogue: Embracing the Big-ME: A Guide to Living
   a Conscious Life 206

Glossary

Throughout this book, you may encounter terms that may be used interchangeably. We encourage you to select the terminology that resonates most with you to enhance your understanding. To create a more personalised and immersive reading experience, you can use the following terms synonymously.

Terminology	Alternative terms and description
The Big-YOU	• Higher self • Universal self • Spirit • Soul • Divine or God • Source droplet or fractal • Deity • Essence • Instinct • Intuition • Internal compass • Life force

	- Gut instinct - Hunch - Inner knowing or guidance - Inner being or voice - Inner wisdom - Breath - Sixth sense (See the seven senses below.) - Cosmic energy - Innate superpower - Inner angel
The Human-YOU	- Human self - Earthly vessel - Avatar - Vessel - Container - Human pot - Human receptacle - Ego or Id
Aware	- Awake - Spiritually awakened - Enlightenment - Discovering nirvana - Bliss - Satori - Understanding
Belief	- Trust - Faith - Confidence

Meditative or meditation	- To think - Contemplate - Serenity - State of calmness - Peace - Untroubled relaxation - Ponder - Relax - Chill out - Stillness - To focus - Connecting with Big-YOU or spirit
Serendipitous	Accidentally, being in the right place at the right time, like bumping into a good friend in an unusual location or finding a hundred-dollar bill on the ground.
Seven senses	The seven senses are as follows: 1. Visual 2. Auditory 3. Smell 4. Taste 5. Touch 6. Knowing 7. Feeling

Purpose	The contract entered into before stepping into the earthly game of things and themes that Big-YOU wants to experience: - • Theme • Mission • Tasks • Goals • Agenda • Interactions or specific events • Aim • Sensory learnings

Context

Context

Hello reader,

I am John, and I would like to explain the focus of this book, which is relevant to many people's current experiences. The phenomenon is often referred to as 'spiritual awakening' or 'spiritual awareness'. Both terms accurately describe the process of becoming more conscious of the larger picture that exists beyond our physical reality.

I do not believe that one suddenly 'wakes up' to this reality. Rather, we become increasingly aware of our connection to a greater construct, a higher presence. You may have already sensed this and are now seeking to understand it better.

In essence, this greater picture involves the existence of a spiritual realm, which is recognised by both religious and spiritual communities, although their perspectives may differ. Our human selves are the vessels for our life force, which is the essence of who we are—The Big-YOU, our spirit, higher self, gut instinct, intuition, or any other term you prefer.

This book aims to examine the workings of this spiritual connection with our human selves, with the ultimate goal of enhancing, refining and maximising our human earthly experience:

- Before it enters the game, the Big-YOU agrees upon the role it will play, the ones it will interact with, that is, its soul family and other spirits and the themes and experiences it wishes to explore to 'grow' as a spirit and for the growth of the spiritual collective.

- The Big-YOU then chooses a human avatar, that is, you. It chooses everything about you as a human—the era in which you exist and your attributes (gender, location, probable lifetime, physical or mental limitations, your preferences—basically, your initial hardware and software programming).

- The Big-YOU then enters the earthly game and starts playing it. The Big-YOU 'sits' both inside the game and outside in the spiritual realm. To make it more realistic, the Big-YOU agrees that the part of it that 'enters' the human avatar will forget who it is for a very important reason. This allows the Big-YOU to have a more immersive, sensory-experiential adventure with all the human senses, such as having the amazing experience of eating chocolate or the thrill of a rollercoaster ride. This forgetfulness also allows the Human-YOU to have free will and do what it desires without the constant direct intervention of the Big-YOU.

- Throughout this lifetime, the only way the Big-YOU and your guides (angels, guardian angel, spirit) can influence the human avatar is through inputs that are not direct, such as the following ones:
    a. 'Internally' through the seven human senses, also known as instinct and intuition.
    b. 'Externally' through the earthly game itself, such as your interactions with humans and animals, your environment, or health issues.
- During this time, most humans live their lives unaware and unawakened to the knowledge of this setup. Many will be fervently against this understanding, which is fine and should be respected because it is their essence's gameplay and experience. They may want and need to have the full immersive unaware experience. You, too, were once in this position.
- Once you have this knowledge and are in an aware and awakened state, together, the Human-YOU and the Big-YOU can begin to have an amazing and rewarding new adventure and experience. It gives you newfound freedom and control you may never have felt before.

The Author's Story

The Author

    Unknown to me, my consciousness has been gradually expanding over the past three to four decades. The global pandemic ignited a profound awakening and awareness, unveiling the existence of a spiritual dimension within me. This revelation marked the beginning of a transformative journey, an adventure into new realms.

    For half a century, I had navigated various earthly experiences with contentment, immersing myself in worldly pursuits and careers as a middle ranking diplomat travelling the world, an IT business consultant, a struggling business owner and working for a logistics company and other corporations in various roles. Little did I know that there lay a dormant spiritual aspect longing to be revealed and to become known to me.

    In the aftermath of the pandemic (2019-21), a profound shift occurred within me. My true self, my Essence, which I have come to refer to as the Big-ME, recognised that it was time for me to awaken to my spiritual identity, my purpose in this lifetime, and my direct connection to the Big-ME. This realisation propelled me into a new earthly game zone, where the new 'awakened state' held infinite possibilities for growth and exploration.

Over the past few years, I have found myself in a period of introspection and growth, with the Big-ME guiding my human experience. I received two fundamental messages from the Big-ME:

- Firstly, the Big-ME has impressed upon me the importance of active listening and attention. In the hustle and bustle of daily existence, I realised I had overlooked this vital skill, leading to missed opportunities for growth and understanding.

- Secondly, the Big-ME emphasised the significance of patience, teaching me that the journey itself is the true adventure and that I should focus on the journey rather than solely on the destination. This valuable lesson has inspired me to embrace each step of life's path with curiosity and anticipation rather than fixating on the end goal.

With these insights in mind, I discovered a new purpose in my human experience—to share the wisdom imparted by my spiritual side with those embarking on their own journey of self-discovery. I wish to share this knowledge without any attachment to the outcome and with the understanding that people will resonate with the message when they are ready to receive it.

I aim to provide a resource for individuals seeking guidance, inspiration, and assistance along their personal paths through various mediums—including this book, videos, workshops and speaking at conferences.

Everyone has a unique path to learning and growth. There isn't just one right way to access information or wisdom. While the core principles may be universal, how we understand and apply them is deeply personal.

From my unique viewpoint and perception, I aim to provide a practical understanding of how to live and curate your best life. I hope this information will be beneficial to you on your new journey and beyond.

My Awakening to Awareness

Soul Agreement

My journey of self-discovery commenced when I embarked on a quest to unravel the mysteries of the universe and my own existence of 'Who am I' and 'What is my true purpose in life?'.

Previously to this and for as long as I can remember, there existed a profound emptiness within me, a gaping void that no earthly pursuit could fill. It wasn't a matter of circumstance; friends, family, achievements, even travel couldn't touch it. It was like a deep, intrinsic longing that I couldn't understand, a gnawing sense of being different, not being able to fit in.

The despair was so consuming that I almost gave up, resigning myself to the belief that happiness was simply out of reach. I learned to ignore the emptiness and imagine it wasn't there, carrying on with my life. The emptiness was always in the back of my mind, and I felt particularly lonely during periods of isolation. I thought friendships and crowds would solve the problem, but they never did.

Even during seemingly joyful periods, the void remained, a constant reminder of my disconnect with the modern world and my place within it.

There was a time when I became a diplomat and travelled the world in the early 2000s, I realised that I was living a carefree life with decisions being made by others about where I would go geographically around the globe to work. Those 15 years were the happiest times of my life, and I later realised that it was my spiritual side guiding me through that period. However, as I was unaware of this and living my human life I decided to move back into corporate life and worked in various industries all trying to help others, but I soon realised that none of those jobs filled the void I was still trying to ignore.

Then came the pandemic. For many, it served as a catalyst, awakening their spiritual side, connecting them to their true selves. For me, it was the final push, the moment I truly acknowledged the deep-seated void and the need to address it. This exhibited physically, as a persistent and perplexing cough that had plagued me for years.

Initially, this cough was incessant. It occurred every few minutes, and I would go into involuntary spasms. Recurring coughing fits throughout the day left me exhausted and distressed. Despite countless medical consultations, scans, and tests, conventional medicine failed to provide an explanation or solution.

After the upheaval of the pandemic and my involvement in the response efforts, I resolved to take some time out for myself by booking a holiday in Thailand. A close friend suggested consulting a psychic, so I planned to do that on my holiday.

I scheduled a virtual session. During the Zoom call, we delved into my health concerns. The psychic inquired about the onset of my cough. I recalled that it had emerged while I worked in Venezuela in the early 2000s.

Instantly, the psychic's behaviour shifted. 'I understand,' she whispered. Weaving an intricate narrative, she told me where the cough originated and why I had it.

I was a conquistador[1], a Spanish soldier, in another lifetime. I was sent to Venezuela as part of the invading army with orders from my commanding officers to clear out a village. As part of this clearance, I set the village on fire with all the inhabitants still in there.

When I heard her narrate these life events, I was shocked to learn that I had committed murder, even if it was in another lifetime. It wasn't just murder. It was mass murder.

That wasn't the strangest thing. She then informed me that when our spirit or essence inhabits another human form and lifetime, it tends to return to areas on the planet it had lived in during other lifetimes. This being the case, one of the strong desires of the Big-ME was to return to Venezuela.

So, in this life, I was sent to Caracas, Venezuela, and lived in a lovely apartment on the same site as the burnt-out village. Thus, this was hallowed ground. As I was living in the same location as the village and the original inhabitants, their spirits, still hanging around the area, realised that I was the same spirit. They decided to try to give me the same experience of choking as I had given them by causing me to have breathing problems. So, I began to have an intense, debilitating cough. That's how it physically happened to me in this lifetime.

It was such a bizarre story that I thought there must be some semblance of reality to it.

I told the psychic that I did not mean to be a mass murderer in that lifetime. I asked her what I could do to bring peace to those spirits.

---

1   A Conquistador (English: Conqueror; Conquistadores, or Conquistadors) was a Spanish or Portuguese soldier, explorer, and adventurer.[1][2] The Conquistadors invaded and conquered much of the Americas and the Philippines Islands and other islands in Asia Pacific.

"We'll just change your past," she said. "Instead of being ordered to eradicate this village, you arrived in Venezuela, met a Venezuelan woman, left the military, became a farmer, had a family, and lived by the coast. The whole aspect of you eradicating a village is not in your current or the other timeline anymore."

I asked her if it was as simple as that.

She said it was. She also said that peace was made with the villagers' spirits, that the timeline was changed, and my cough would virtually disappear in six months to two years.

Which it has. I came to understand that there was an agreement between the Big-ME and the villagers' spirits that the cough would be a catalyst and the start of my awakening process. The contract was now complete between the two sets of spirits transcending the two lifetimes.

Looking back now, a transformative trip to Thailand became a turning point in my life. It forced me to confront who I was and what I was doing with my life. It was like a reawakening, reconnecting me with my 'Big-ME," as I came to call it. I also realised that this moment of awareness was not a random occurrence, but a preordained juncture in my current lifetime, orchestrated by a higher power – the Big-ME. This awakening paved the way for a life enhancing journey of self-discovery.

Over the resulting years, I have explored various spiritual practices, including past or other life regression (Beyond Quantum Healing Practitioner) and accessing the akashic or universal records, these are forms of therapy that introduced me formally to the concept of my Big-ME and how to connect with our spiritual side for guidance and well-being.

This experience opened my eyes to a whole new world of understanding, a connection between the Human-ME and the spiritual me or the Big-ME. I also realised that the former concept of my purpose in life that of trying to help and assist others was transformed to helping others to connect with their innate self – 'The Big-YOU'.

This book is a testament to that journey, a guide for others seeking to embark on their own personal quest for self-discovery. It's important to remember that everyone's journey is unique; my perspective is just one among many. Exploring different viewpoints and embracing the multitude of spiritual paths will ultimately lead to a deeper understanding of ourselves.

Let us embark on this journey together.

How to Use This Book

Embrace this book as a trusted companion, a guide to help you navigate the intricacies of life on Earth. Delve into its pages with an open mind, seeking inspiration and wisdom that sparks your inner flame.

When you encounter information that aligns with your experiences and beliefs, embrace it. Let it ignite your understanding and fuel your journey. However, when you come across perspectives that do not resonate with your truth, do not force yourself to accept them. Instead, let them gently pass you by, respecting your unique path.

Remember, the insights shared within these pages are the author's interpretation and perspective. They serve as a lens through which you can explore the complexities of life, but ultimately, the choices you make are your own.

Use this guidebook as a compass, guiding you towards the most authentic path towards your Big-YOU.

Chapter 1
The Human Life Experience (HLE) Model

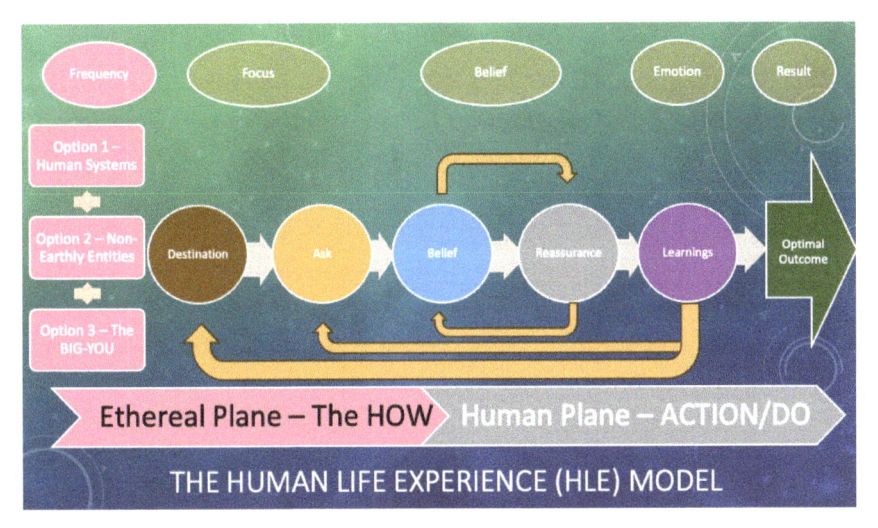

Figure 1

YOUR DUAL NATURE: HUMAN AND SPIRIT

A profound duality exists within us—two interconnected parts of a single being. This book presents a human perspective that explores the symbiotic relationship between our earthly selves (Human-YOU) and our higher selves (Big-YOU).

We can navigate our human journey with greater purpose and fulfilment by harnessing this connection which can be represented by using the above Human Life Experience (HLE) Model (Figure 1).

At first glance, the HLE model may seem intricate. Its purpose is to give a graphic overview of this duality and show how we can use techniques and formulas to show the interaction and understanding between the two interconnected parts of ourselves.

As we delve deeper into this book, an understanding emerges. From the vantage point of our human selves, we see ourselves as actors in a grand play called life. Yet, ultimately, it is the Big-YOU who holds the reins. It utilises the Human-YOU as an avatar, an instrument through which it experiences the earthly realm.

This merging allows the Big-YOU to fully immerse itself in the highs and lows of life. Human experiences are the building blocks of its growth and evolution. Therefore, the events that unfold in our human lives must be considered in the context of the Big-YOU's overarching purpose and plan.

As we navigate our earthly existence, it is essential to cultivate a harmonious connection with our Big-YOU. By aligning our actions and aspirations with their divine wisdom, we unlock the potential to create a fulfilling and meaningful human life that serves both the Human-YOU and the Big-YOU within us.

This book is a roadmap and a guidebook, one among many, to help you discover and live your best life. There are countless teachers and resources out there, all offering unique perspectives and valuable insights. Find those that resonate with you and explore their wisdom to enhance your personal growth and spiritual understanding and awareness.

I have shared what I believe is essential for awakening you to your full potential. The rest is up to you. My goal is to guide you towards self-awareness, clarity about your purpose and an understanding of the human experience. By applying these principles, you can design and curate a life that aligns both with your individual aspirations and the Big-YOU's greater purpose.

This book offers a practical approach to navigating the earthly journey. Embrace the adventure and remember that you are infinitely capable of creating a life filled with joy and fulfilment. Have fun and enjoy the adventure that awaits you.

Chapter 2
The 3.5.1. Method

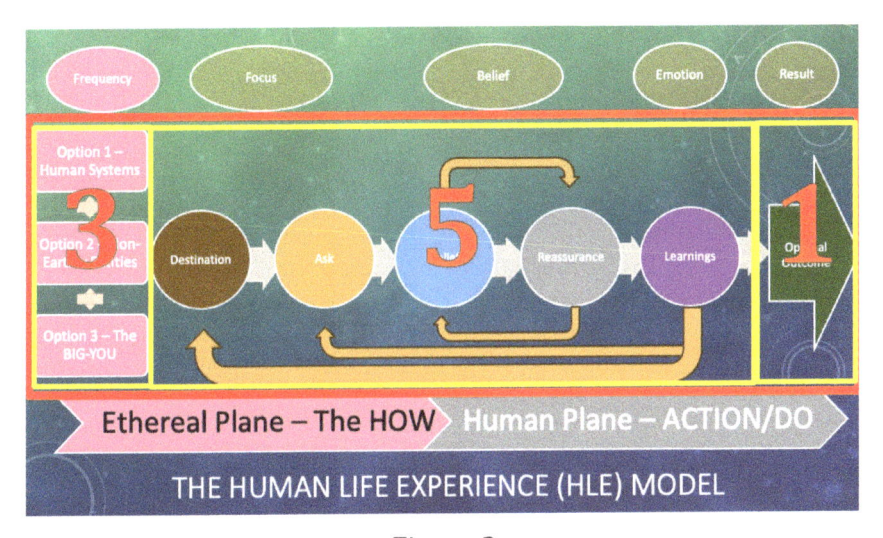

Figure 2

Unlocking Your Desired Outcome: A Three-Part Approach

This chapter explores a powerful methodology, which I have termed the **3.5.1. Method** (Figure 2). It can help you achieve your desired outcome. Forged through years of personal testing and refinement, this method has proven effective in my own life, and I encourage you to try it for yourself.

Part One: Connecting With the Spirit Realm

The journey begins with establishing a connection to the spirit realm. This is your unique path to tapping into a higher level of guidance and inspiration. We will examine three distinct methods and options available for you to forge this connection, allowing you to choose the approach that resonates most deeply with your human experience.

Part Two: Five Pillars of Success

Once connected, we move to the five pillars that form the foundation for achieving your optimal outcome. These are the essential mechanics that will guide you towards your goal. Each pillar has a feedback loop and represents a vital step in the process, working in synergy to create a powerful force for positive change.

Part Three: The Optimal Outcome

Finally, we explore the concept of the optimal outcome. While it might not always align with your initial human desires, it represents the outcome that truly serves your highest good, encompassing both your human and spiritual aspirations. Rest assured, this Big-YOU desired outcome is always in your best interests, even if it appears different from what you initially envisioned.

Let us embark on this journey together and delve into the profound methodology that will unlock your potential and guide you towards your optimal outcome.

PART ONE: THE THREE OPTIONS—TAPPING INTO THE DIVINE

Connection to Ethereal - 3 Options

In spiritual exploration, three distinct options exist to serve as conduits between the human vessel and the spirit world. Each method grants you access to the realm of spirits and enables you to communicate with them.

The options are interchangeable, offering equal effectiveness in facilitating the selection and creation of the timeline that individuals experience consciously and subconsciously throughout their lifetime. While all three options are valid, each individual may prefer one or employ different options at various stages of their life journey.

All the options involve collaboration with the spirit realm to achieve the desired outcomes and manifest the intended results.

This book primarily employs option three as it aligns with my, the authors favourite method of communication with the spirit realm.

Options one and two utilise similar techniques, methodologies, and principles, ensuring effectiveness regardless of the choice made by the reader.

It is worth noting that other options may exist beyond those presented here. I do not discount these but do not cover them because of my limited awareness of them.

The key to all the options is 'belief'. If you trust in the power of these various options, modalities and techniques, they can empower you to create the life you desire.

3.1. The Human-Self's Viewpoint

Let us talk about the first option you can use to curate your life. This is from the vantage point of utilising human-centred practices and modalities. The approach leverages earthly techniques to achieve the desired outcomes, embracing a spectrum of methods, such as the following:

- Meditation and Rituals: Cultivating mindfulness and creating meaningful ceremonies.
- Symbols and Repetition: Harnessing the power of imagery and consistent practice.
- Practices and Processes: Utilising proven methods to achieve goals.
- Numerology and Tarot: Exploring the symbolic meanings within numbers and cards.
- Spells and Star Charts: Engaging in symbolic actions and aligning with cosmic energies.
- Astrology and Feng Shui: Drawing insights from celestial bodies and optimising your environment.
- Artifacts and Self-Help Tools: Utilising tangible objects and practical guides.
- Mantras and Management Speak: Harnessing the power of words, strategies and positive affirmation.

This approach is grounded in the human perspective and can be profoundly effective.

Whether you are drawn to the spiritual side of things or are simply seeking practical tools for a fulfilling life, embracing earthly techniques can be a valuable path.

3.2. The Non-Earthly Entities' Viewpoint

This second approach, which I call 'utilising non-human entities,' finds its roots in many spiritual traditions, including religions, sects, and personal practices. It involves seeking guidance and support from a spectrum of beings beyond the human realm, such as the following ones:

- Guardian and Archangels: Protective spirits assigned to individuals in the earthly realm.
- Soul Family: Spirits connected to you through past lives or shared spiritual journeys.
- Other Spirits: Entities residing in the ethereal realm, potentially offering wisdom or assistance.
- Deities: Powerful beings worshipped in various religions, often seen as creators or rulers of specific domains.
- Ascended Masters: Highly evolved beings who have attained enlightenment and offer guidance.
- Extra-Terrestrial Beings: Intelligent beings originating from other planets, potentially sharing knowledge or insights.

This connection to the non-human realm can be fostered through various practices, including the following ones:

- Prayer: Connecting with spirit.
- Channelling: Allowing spirits to communicate through a person's body.
- Psychic Work: Utilising extrasensory abilities to perceive and interact with the non-physical world.

- Mediumship: Connecting with deceased spirits and relaying their messages.
- Regressions and Other Forms of Meditation: Connecting with spirits and their other lifetimes and relaying their messages.

You can undertake these practices by yourself or through others' guidance.

By trusting in the power of these entities and embracing their guidance, individuals can experience profound transformation and achieve their desired outcomes.

3.3. The Big-YOU's Viewpoint

The third option for navigating life lies within our innate spiritual selves. This isn't about dogma or religion but about connecting with the deepest fountain of wisdom and intuition that resides within each of us.

Think of it as a collaboration between the Human-YOU and the Big-YOU—your Higher Self, your intuition, life force and essence. This powerful alliance can guide you towards the desired outcomes in life.

This connection is cultivated through conscious awareness and trust. We have all experienced this intuition throughout our lives. That feeling you get when you meet someone new, a sense of comfort or unease, is your inner voice speaking. The same applies to entering a new place—that gut feeling of whether it is welcoming or gives you a sense of foreboding. This 'sixth sense' is a vital tool in navigating life's complexities.

We empower ourselves by consciously listening through our senses and trusting this inner wisdom. It becomes a key component in curating our experiences and making choices that align with our true selves.

Your instinct and intuition are always 100 percent correct for you. This is the Big-YOU communicating with the Human-YOU, always acting in your highest and best interests and guiding you towards the most favourable outcomes.

Having the Belief

The biggest hurdle with the three options is having the belief that the option you are drawn to, and use will bring you the knowledge and the certainty that it is working for you. This is the key to what I will be discussing in the following pages.

What's the difference Between "I know" and "I believe"?

There's a subtle but fundamental difference between knowing something and believing something.

When you know something, it comes without a doubt. There is a level of certainty and conviction due to verifiable testing done by yourself or others. It is about a set of facts, and there is sound analytical reasoning behind it. Knowing is connected to knowledge, which is more a reflection of the way things work and the specific details.

When you believe something, it acknowledges more openness and room for interpretation. It suggests an opinion and that you have drawn a certain conclusion and will defend it, but it is still negotiable. Beliefs are assumptions that we make about the world. New information could conflict with what you believe, and you will have to incorporate that into the next version of your understanding.

What is important to mention about belief, though, is there is a lot of passion behind it. There is more of a wanting or longing behind a belief. You are invested in it, and you feel like whatever it is that you believe impacts you. It is more emotional.

When your action comes from a level of belief, there is doubt and emotional passion behind such action.

When your action comes from a level of knowing, there is 100 percent conviction, certainty, and calmness behind such action.

Why I Prefer Option 3

I find myself gravitating towards option three—listening to my intuition, the Big-ME. The preference stems both from my inclinations and my understanding of human nature.

From a practical standpoint, I believe that the human body, devoid of its spirit or life force (death), is merely a physical shell. It is our Higher-Self, or Big-ME, that orchestrates our manifestations, energy shifts, and the apparent 'luck' that shapes our lives.

When our human self and Higher-Self align harmoniously, we can co-create an extraordinary earthly experience. This symbiotic connection fosters a profound understanding of our purpose and empowers us to navigate life's challenges with grace and wisdom.

Ultimately, the most effective option to connect with the Divine is the one that resonates most strongly with you. Whether you choose to rely on one of the options or a combination of all three or explore other approaches, the key is to find a strategy that aligns with your values and beliefs.

PART TWO: FIVE PILLARS FOR CURATING OPTIMAL OUTCOMES

Let us talk about the five pillars or steps for curating the best outcome that you want for anything, whether it is your life's purposes, family, love life, business, employment, friends, accumulating earthly material gains, travelling or whatever else that 'you' desire to do during this earthly game.

The five pillars are as follows:

1. What is your destination?
2. Asking for your desire in the present tense.
3. Belief in the process.
4. Obtaining reassurance and testing the process.
5. Learnings and insights.

5.1. Destination

Destination

We often start our life journeys with a destination in mind. A specific job, a dream location, or a desired achievement. These ambitions can be powerful motivators, guiding us towards our goals. However, focusing solely on the destination can limit our potential. It is like setting out on a road trip with a rigid itinerary, missing the hidden gems and unexpected detours that make the journey truly memorable.

Imagine your life as a grand adventure, a vast landscape waiting to be explored. You, the Human-YOU, are the driver and the vehicle, experiencing the world firsthand. But there is another part of you, the Big-YOU, who operates like a powerful GPS navigation system. While you focus on the road ahead, the Big-YOU has access to the entire map, seeing all the possibilities and knowing the best routes to achieve not just your goals, but also a life that exceeds your wildest dreams.

Think of it like playing a racing game. The player (the Big-YOU) selects the vehicle (the Human-YOU) equipped with full self-driving capabilities. The player has access to the entire track and all the other drivers and knows the game's secrets from start to finish. Yet, the player chooses to immerse itself in the game, momentarily forgetting its omniscient perspective.

This amnesia allows for a more immersive and authentic sensory experience, a thrilling adventure that feels genuine and real. The Big-YOU chooses to relinquish direct control due to this amnesia, allowing the Human-YOU the freedom to explore and make choices. However, the Big-YOU whispers guidance, nudging you towards experiences that will enrich your life. It might suggest taking a scenic detour, encountering unexpected challenges, or even experiencing a thrilling crash, all for the purpose of personal growth and a deeper understanding of itself and the world.

So, while setting a destination can be a helpful guiding star, it is essential to remember that the true treasure is the journey itself. Embrace the unexpected twists and turns, the moments of joy and sorrow, the challenges and triumphs. Trust the Big-YOU, your internal Sat Nav (satellite navigation), to navigate you towards a life that surpasses your wildest dreams. The true destination isn't just a point on the map but the tapestry of experiences, both planned and unplanned, that make your life extraordinary.

At the core of any journey lies the destination, a guiding star that fuels our actions and aspirations. As we navigate the game of life, it is essential to establish a clear and well-defined destination to ensure a meaningful and purposeful path.

To effectively determine our destination, we can utilise the following 'Five Ws':

1. What: What do we aspire to achieve? What is the ultimate goal that we seek to accomplish?
2. Where: Where do we envision ourselves ending up? What environment or situation do we strive to create for ourselves?
3. When: By what timeline do we aim to reach our destination? Is it a short-term objective or a long-term aspiration?
4. Who: Who will be our companions or collaborators on this journey? Who will offer support, encouragement and a sense of community?
5. Why: Ultimately, why do we embark on this path? What is the deeper purpose and motivation behind our actions?

Addressing these questions will help us define our destination with precision. However, it is important to remember that the 'How' of achieving our goals falls under the purview of the Big-YOU, the wise and strategic navigator and co-pilot within us.

Through collaboration between the Human-YOU and the Big-YOU, we can ensure that we not only reach our destination but also experience growth and transformation along the way. With its understanding of our true desires and aspirations, the Big-YOU will guide our choices and actions, ultimately leading us to a better and more fulfilling outcome than we could have imagined.

5.2. Asking

Ask

Navigating towards a desired outcome requires more than just setting a goal. Once you have established your destination, the next crucial step is 'asking for guidance in the present tense as if the journey has been completed.' This act of communication is like entering your destination into a GPS, providing the necessary direction for your journey.

Just as a blank GPS screen won't guide you, failing to ask for guidance will leave your path unclear. By expressing your desires to your Big-YOU—your inner self—you unlock the potential for guidance. This guidance can manifest itself in different ways—from one of your senses, such as your intuitive feelings and knowing, to external forces, such as people who offer advice or situations that redirect you towards a better path.

Imagine a dog leading its owner on an adventure. By allowing the dog to guide them, the owner may discover unexpected, wondrous paths. Similarly, by being open to the guidance of your Big-YOU, you can access unexpected opportunities and embark on fulfilling journeys.

The act of asking for guidance is a vital bridge between your aspiration and its realisation. It empowers you to tap into your inner wisdom and allows the universe to conspire in your favour, leading you towards your desired destination

The concepts of time and space are constructs created by humans to enhance the immersive experience of the Big-YOU through the Human-YOU in this earthly game. The Big-YOU resides both within the game—our earthly reality—and outside it, in the ethereal realm where only the present moment exists.

A way to understand time is to imagine a streaming service on your TV, offering a vast library of content. Each channel represents a different reality, with past, present and future events unfolding simultaneously. As the viewer, the Human-YOU, you have the ability to select any channel and immerse yourself in its content. The Human-YOU chooses to focus on any channel or genre you wish to explore and be immersed in the subject matter. We will discuss this in greater detail later in the book. The Big-YOU then orchestrates the mechanics of immersing the Human-YOU into the chosen channel.

This understanding is crucial because it reveals that the Big-YOU and the Human-YOU exist in a static present while they are presented with all possible realities. So, it is essential to express desires in the present tense, knowing that the desired outcome will manifest itself at the appropriate time when all the necessary conditions align.

This concept was explored in the 2006 film 'The Secret'[2] using the example of parking a car. When you believe wholeheartedly that a parking space will be available near your destination, the Big-YOU orchestrates events to ensure it happens. In essence, you are choosing a specific reality from the infinite possibilities available within the streaming service of life.

---

2   https://en.wikipedia.org/wiki/The_Secret_(2006_film)

You would state, "When I go in a car, there will always be parking space for me at or very close to my destination. I am open to surprises that may optimise the outcome of this request. Thank you."

So, ask for the version with a car parking space at or very close to your destination and be open to better options, such as a valet service at your destination.

5.3. Belief

Belief

Belief in the process and your respective roles is the next pillar.

As discussed above, we have an invisible sat nav co-pilot, the Big-YOU. Its role is to navigate the path towards our desired outcomes through an intricate mechanism that transcends our conscious understanding.

Belief plays a pivotal role in this mechanism, encompassing two key aspects:

1. Passion and Emotion: Belief fuels our actions with immense passion and emotion driving us towards our goals.
2. Openness to Outcomes: Belief allows us to embrace the unknown, trusting our Big-YOU that the outcome will surpass our human limitations and dreams.

The Human-YOU serves as the avatar in this earthly journey, responsible for executing the actions that lead to our destination. Our free will allows us to disregard guidance from the Big-YOU, but such actions often lead to unforeseen consequences. But that is fine and is part of the adventure. There is no blame or retribution from the Big-YOU, just love and guidance for you to return to the path of the Big-YOU's purpose.

Harmony arises when we align with the guidance of the Big-YOU. It possesses a comprehensive understanding of our life's path and seeks our well-being. By listening and acting in accordance with its guidance, we create a harmonious experience filled with joy and fulfilment.

The Big-YOU has chosen us as the ideal human avatar for its journey. It knows every facet of our being, making us uniquely suited to play this role.

When we embrace belief and trust in the process, our Big-YOU allows us to flow effortlessly through life. We navigate challenges and embrace opportunities with confidence, knowing that the Big-YOU has our best and highest interests at heart.

5.4. Seek Reassurance or Proof

Testing and Reassurance

In the realm of human understanding, the concept of a higher self can seem illogical. We question its existence due to our limited perception, doubting the possibility of a guiding force beyond our physical experience. However, there exists a simple solution—seek reassurance.

Our higher self, the Big-YOU, possesses infinite love and a desire to guide us. We are like a stray dog with trust issues, requiring consistent reassurance to foster a bond of trust and mutual connection. Repeatedly asking for proof or reassurance from our Big-YOU will never be met with resentment or impatience.

Through patient reassurance, we, too, can embrace the presence of our Big-YOU.

Begin by asking for small yet tangible signs of its guidance, such as "Explicitly, show me something amazing today so that I know it is you."

Witnessing the fulfilment of such requests will strengthen your belief and understanding.

Over time, as you cultivate trust in the Big-YOU, the bond you share will deepen. You will experience a sense of support and guidance, knowing that you are not alone in navigating your life journey. Like a loyal companion, the Big-YOU will always be present, providing reassurance and illuminating your path.

5.5. Listen, Be Adaptable and Go with the Flow

THE BIG-YOU

Learnings

You will encounter learnings, insights and revelations along the way, but be prepared for surprises. Embrace flexibility and have an open mind, as the path may take unexpected turns, leading you to new and potentially transformative experiences.

These insights are sometimes perceived as setbacks or failures, but more specifically, 'redirections' and initially manifest as subtle whispers or gentle nudges provided to you by the Big-YOU. Ignoring these prompts leads to more assertive manifestations, such as health concerns or significant events, such as financial losses. These experiences can be deeply personal or connected to loved ones, serving as wake-up calls that prompt us to alter our course or acquire invaluable knowledge.

Therefore, the path of least resistance to mitigate these painful lessons involves actively listening, adapting, and allowing ourselves to be guided by our Big-YOU.

The Human-YOU frequently assumes control and focuses on the 'How', which lies outside its purview. True fulfilment arises when we surrender control and embrace the transformative journey itself. Remember, when you are going on a journey, it isn't the destination that is the exciting bit or the adventure. It is the journey itself.

Maintain flexibility, openness, and adaptability, as these qualities enhance the adventure and unlock the potential for the occurrence of even more extraordinary outcomes. Cease the futile attempt to exert control. Instead, embrace the flow of life.

Allow your Big-YOU to guide your experiences and fully immerse yourself in the present moment. By relaxing into the journey and embracing the unknown, you will unlock the true adventure your Big-YOU intended for you.

PART THREE: OPTIMUM DESIRED RESULT OR OUTCOME

Optimal Output

While the optimal outcome may not always align with your initial human desires, it represents the outcome that truly serves your highest good, encompassing both your human and spiritual aspirations. Rest assured, this Big-YOU desired outcome is always in your best interest, even if it appears different from what you initially envisioned.

Embrace Your True Self: The Harmony of the Big-YOU and Human-YOU

Your existence is not merely a random occurrence. The Big-YOU is your true essence, the architect of your life's journey. It possesses an intricate understanding of all your experiences and potential paths.

Upon embarking on this earthly adventure, the Big-YOU carefully selected the Human-YOU as its avatar. The Human-YOU is the physical embodiment through which the Big-YOU interacts with the world. Together, you collaborate to fulfill the Big-YOU's aspirations.

The authentic Human-YOU is aligned with the desires and objectives of the Big-YOU. By embracing this harmony, you cultivate a life characterised by synchronicity, serendipity, and adventure.

Understand that the Human-YOU is not the hero but a vital vessel through which the Big-YOU expresses itself. When you align with the Big-YOU's intentions, your life transforms into a symphony of purpose and execution.

Embrace the deep connection between your Big-YOU and Human-YOU. When the Human-YOU surrenders and collaborates with the Big-YOU, allowing it to guide its decisions, your human desires, purpose, and your optimum outcome perfectly align with the Big-YOU. The collaboration empowers you to live a rich, authentic and deeply rewarding life.

Harnessing the Power of Intention

It is time to put the technique to the test for yourself. Don't simply accept my word. Experience its impact firsthand. Begin modestly, perhaps by requesting favourable weather conditions or help to avoid traffic congestion or a sign. As your confidence grows, expand the scope of your desires.

For instance, I regularly employ this method during extended motorway drives, requesting dry weather conditions. Remarkably, in 99 percent of cases, it remains dry, or if it does rain, it clears up within minutes or miles.

I could dismiss this as coincidence or chance, but I choose to believe that I am actively influencing the weather outcome through my Big-ME by choosing the version and timeline with the most conducive weather and traffic. I am the master of my own destiny and can shape my interactions with life's events.

Remember, utilise the aspects of the 3.5.1. Method that resonate with you the most. Feel free to adapt or incorporate other ideas. Ultimately, this is your life and your experience. Make it uniquely yours by melding it to your preferences.

Chapter 3
The Lucky Formula

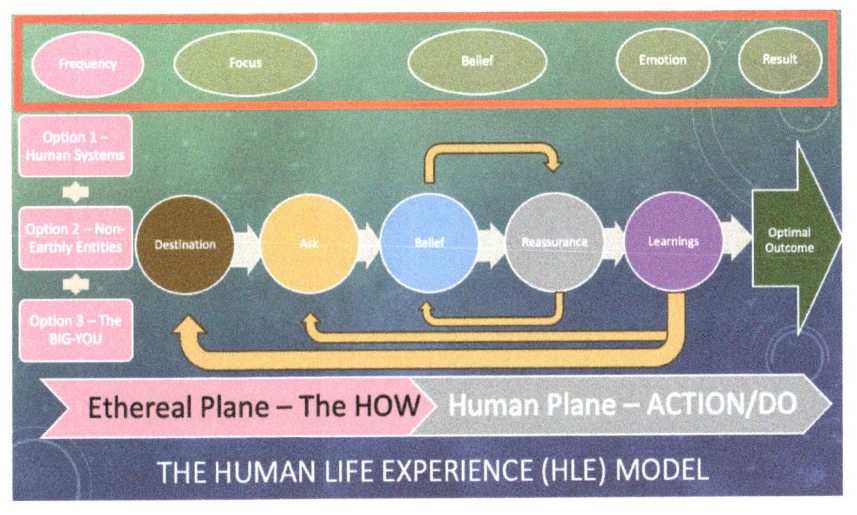

(Figure 3)

OVERVIEW

The Lucky Formula (Figure 3) is a simple overarching explanation of the more in-depth mechanics of the 3.5.1. Method we discussed in Chapter 2, why it works and how it can be used in daily life.

The Human-YOU Role

Focus + Belief creates an emotion or trigger: The Action or Doing

> **Big-YOU Role**
>
> Frequency and Vibration: The How
>
> > **To curate the Optimal Outcome**

WHAT IS THE LUCKY FORMULA FOR THE HUMAN-YOU?

1. Focus on what you desire.
2. Believe in the optimal outcome for your desire.

Have you ever noticed how effortlessly our desires manifest when we truly believe in them? It is like ordering food at a restaurant—we expect the meal to be prepared and delivered to us. This intrinsic trust in the process, coupled with the act of placing the order, sets the wheels in motion.

Unknowingly, we tap into this powerful dynamic throughout our lives. From pursuing a dream job to building strong relationships, our subconscious minds often guide us towards our desired outcomes. Now, imagine harnessing this innate ability consciously.

The 3.5.1. Method acts as a blueprint for this intentional manifestation. By focusing on what we want, believing in its realisation, having an emotional response and taking concrete action, we create a potent synergy that propels us closer to our goals.

Think of it as unlocking your inner potential, the Big-YOU, and collaborating with the Human-YOU to manifest a fulfilling life. This conscious application of belief and action empowers us to shape our reality and navigate towards a future filled with purpose and abundance.

WHY DOES THE LUCKY FORMULA WORK?

As discussed, the concept of the Big-YOU and the Human-YOU posits that an ethereal and spiritual aspect of our being, the Big-YOU, orchestrates our life experiences for our human selves, the Human-YOU. This relationship operates through a mechanism known as the Lucky Formula.

While it has a localised presence in our earthly realm, the Big-YOU also resides on a higher spiritual plane where it possesses infinite knowledge and power. To enable us to fully immerse ourselves in the sensory and experiential aspects of our existence, it has, however, chosen to suppress its omniscience by forgetting itself for our lifetime. Is it possible to describe the sensory experience of eating chocolate from a theoretical point of view? One needs to 'live' the sensations.

The Lucky Formula serves as the conduit through which the Big-YOU interprets our desires and intentions—as expressed by the Human-YOU—and translates them into tangible outcomes. The Human-YOU provides guidance, direction and initiative to the Big-YOU within the realm of physical actions and decisions.

The Big-YOU leverages its access to cosmic insights and the vastness of the spiritual realm to orchestrate events and shape circumstances that align with our aspirations. This process is akin to the Big-YOU acting as a cosmic curator, designing a life adventure tailored to the desires of the Human-YOU.

By understanding the nature of the Big-YOU and the role of the lucky formula, we gain insight into the mechanisms that shape our lives. Harnessing the power of our Human-YOU's desires and aligning them with the guidance of our Big-YOU allows us to create a harmonious and liberating existence.

THE TWO-PART SYMPHONY OF EXISTENCE: HUMAN AND BIG-YOU

Our earthly experience is a complex dance, a symphony performed by two distinct yet interconnected entities—the Human-YOU and the Big-YOU. The Human-YOU is the physical embodiment, the avatar we inhabit during this lifetime. The Big-YOU, on the other hand, represents the non-physical essence, the life force that animates us.

The undeniable truth of our mortality underscores this duality. When we die, our Human-YOU, the physical vessel, decomposes, returning to the earth's elements. Yet, something endures—the Big-YOU, the life force—which moves on.

This realisation reveals the Big-YOU's role as the orchestrator of our earthly journey. It is the unseen hand that guides our experiences, influencing our luck, shaping our energy, and ultimately curating the tapestry of our lives. The Big-YOU chose this specific Human-YOU as its avatar, recognising its potential to embody a particular set of experiences. It holds a complete understanding of your essence, every version of you, making you the ideal vessel for this lifetime.

While the Human-YOU possesses free will and can explore various paths, its desires often align with the Big-YOU's intentions because these actions make you happy and fulfill your desires. The synergy allows for a rich tapestry of experiences in which the Big-YOU's overarching goals intertwine with the Human-YOU's individual passions and aspirations. Yet, if the Human-YOU strays too far from the Big-YOU's intended course, subtle nudges and more forceful guidance may appear, leading you back towards the path of intended growth and transformation. Ultimately, even near-death experiences can act as powerful reminders to realign with the Big-YOU's plan.

The Human-YOU is crucial to this interplay. It acts as the sensory conduit, allowing the Big-YOU to fully immerse itself in the earthly experience. The Human-YOU's actions and choices shape the journey, creating a narrative that resonates with both parties. Whether it is pursuing athletic excellence, creating art, nurturing others, or exploring the depth of thoughts, the Human-YOU's passions are often reflections of the Big-YOU's desires to experience the full spectrum of earthly life. Some religions call this doing 'God's work', but in actuality, it is the aligning of symbiotic interests.

In essence, the Human-YOU and the Big-YOU are inextricably linked, two parts of a single symphony. They co-create an intricate dance of life, where the Big-YOU orchestrates the grand plan, and the Human-YOU embodies its essence, navigating the earthly stage with a unique blend of free will and divine guidance. Through this collaboration, both entities participate in a journey of growth, discovery, and, ultimately, a serendipitous, shared potential.

ROLES AND RESPONSIBILITIES

Doing the Action Part

(Your Human Role)

The Lucky Formula isn't about forcing luck but embracing the natural flow of life. It thrives on the mundane, the everyday 'actions' that make up our existence, such as shopping, cleaning, relaxing, connecting with others, preparing meals, socialising with friends and family, exercising, commuting and working. These seemingly ordinary tasks become the canvas upon which serendipity paints its masterpiece.

While you focus on the practicalities of your daily life, a higher, more intuitive part of yourself—the Big-YOU—works behind the scenes. This intuitive force observes, analyses, and guides you towards your optimal outcome. It weaves opportunities, synchronicities, and seemingly coincidental events into your experience, all in perfect timing.

The key lies in attentiveness—being present to the whispers of your intuition. Notice those subtle nudges, those unexpected doors opening, those serendipitous encounters. Act on them, even if they seem insignificant at first. This is how the Big-YOU communicates, guiding you towards implementing your deepest desires.

By trusting the process, surrendering to the flow of life and embracing the mundane, you open yourself to a world of possibilities. The Lucky Formula isn't about chasing luck. It is about acknowledging its presence every day and embracing and attracting all the opportunities and the version of the future that you both wish to explore.

Navigating The Timelines: Directing Your Focus

(Your Human Role)

Imagine your life as a vast streaming service offering endless possibilities. Every choice, every interest and every action you take opens a new channel, a new timeline, a new version of events. This journey is orchestrated by the Big-YOU, a powerful, unseen force that aligns with your deepest desires, guiding you towards experiences that resonate with your joint purpose.

The Big-YOU operates both consciously and subconsciously. When you actively pursue a passion, like politics, painting, singing or writing, you consciously signal your interest. This attracts opportunities, experiences, and connections that enrich your understanding and expertise in that field. You are essentially tuning into a specific channel in the streaming service of life, exploring that genre in greater depth.

However, even when you are unaware, the Big-YOU continues to work in the background, subtly nudging you towards experiences that align with your soul's purpose. It is like a skilled curator presenting you with a curated selection of opportunities based on your underlying desires.

Think of it as a game. The Big-YOU, the player, watches the Human-YOU, the avatar, navigate the earthly realm. This 'game' is constantly unfolding, presenting you with new opportunities and inputs. Your attention, 'your focus', determines the channels you choose to explore.

The Big-YOU, however, is not passive. It always guides you back towards the ideal path if you stray. This is the power of your gut instinct. A gentle nudge and a whisper of intuition encourage you to return to your true course. Thanks to your free will, you are free to ignore or embrace this inner compass. However, the stronger your interest, the louder the Big-YOU's nudges become.

Therefore, by focusing on what truly interests you, consciously or unconsciously, you are essentially choosing the channels you want to explore in the vast streaming service of your life. Each channel and each timeline offers unique experiences and lessons that help you evolve and experience your purpose. This continues until you get to the point where you are no longer interested in that subject, and you no longer focus on it.

Belief: The Keystone of Your Reality

(Your Human Role)

Belief plays a pivotal role in shaping our lives, encompassing the intentions, emotions, and unwavering desires that guide our actions. It serves as a potent signal to the universe, indicating our aspirations and inviting their manifestation.

Belief sets in motion a process just as we do when we order food at a restaurant. We trust that our order has been received and that the desired outcome will be delivered. We do not incessantly question the status of our order. Instead, we anticipate its arrival with unwavering conviction and a salivating mouth.

In the same way, when we hold a strong belief, we rely on the universe to respond to it. It may take time for our desires to materialise, but we should not doubt their eventual fulfilment. Just as the restaurant will keep us informed of any delays, the universe will provide subtle signs and synchronicities to reassure us that our aspirations are on their way.

Therefore, embrace belief as the foundation on which you build your desired reality. Set clear intentions, infuse them with emotion, and trust that the universe will align with your vision. Allow your beliefs to guide your actions and decisions and remain steadfast in your conviction that your dreams will come to fruition. It is through belief that you activate the power within you to manifest your dreams into reality.

Emotions: The Trigger Event

(Your Human Role)

Emotions are an intrinsic part of the human experience arising from our cognitive processes. When we focus on a particular thought or sensory input, our brain interprets it, resulting in an emotional response. These emotions, in turn, trigger a release of chemical messengers within our bodies, which subsequently evoke feelings.

Following the initial emotional response, the cumulative effect of these feelings fuses into moods. Moods represent a more sustained emotional state, often characterised by their intensity and duration. They can range from positive emotions, such as joy and contentment to negative emotions, such as sadness and anger, and exert a significant influence on our thoughts, actions and well-being.

Emotions serve as valuable signals that guide our behaviour and help us navigate our social and environmental surroundings. By understanding and managing our emotions, we can enhance our resilience, build stronger relationships and live more fulfilling lives.

Some forms and types of emotions are as follows:

- Admiration
- Adoration
- Anger
- Aesthetic appreciation
- Amusement
- Anxiety and worry
- Awe
- Awkwardness
- Boredom
- Calmness
- Confusion
- Contempt
- Craving
- Disgust
- Empathy
- Entrancement
- Envy
- Excitement and anticipation
- Fear and dread

- Guilt
- Hate
- Horror
- Interest
- Joy
- Nostalgia
- Pity
- Pride
- Romance
- Sadness
- Satisfaction
- Sexual desire
- Shame
- Shyness
- Surprise
- Sympathy
- Triumph
- Trust

Emotions are not simply fleeting feelings, but complex biochemical reactions triggered by our interpretation of our experiences. Our remarkably efficient brains can identify a stimulus within a mere quarter of a second, swiftly initiating the release of emotion-inducing chemicals. These chemicals flood our bodies, creating a feedback loop between our minds and physical selves.

Importantly, emotions themselves carry no inherent value—good or bad. It is the Human-YOU, our conscious self, that assigns meaning to these chemical reactions. A surprise, for instance, becomes a good or bad experience only through our personal interpretation.

Emotions act as signposts, guiding our Big-YOU—the core of our being—towards the experiences we desire to explore further. Consider them the clicking or pressing of the remote control of our life's TV, where each press of a button, that is, each emotion, accesses a different channel, a different version of our reality.

By acknowledging and depersonalising our emotional responses, we can choose to observe rather than be overwhelmed. This conscious choice signals the Big-YOU that we are not interested in further exploration of that particular channel, effectively preventing us from becoming engrossed in its drama and storyline.

Ultimately, the presence or absence of an emotional response lies within our control. This awareness empowers us to curate the life we desire, steering clear of unwanted channels and tuning into those that resonate with our deepest desires.

Observe the lives of individuals who are easily swayed by their emotions. Teenagers, for example, often experience rapid shifts in mood, leading to unpredictable and tumultuous lives with rapidly changing timelines. This chaotic dance of emotions results from their inability to navigate and control these internal signals, creating a whirlwind impact on themselves and those around them.

By understanding the interplay between triggers, chemicals and our own interpretations, we can gain mastery over our emotional landscape. This knowledge empowers us to navigate the complex terrain of our inner world, choosing to engage with some experiences and gracefully decline others, creating a life that aligns with our truest selves.

Vibration and Frequency: The How Part

(Your Essence's Role)

As a human being, you don't need to concern yourself with the intricacies of vibration and frequency. This task falls to your Big-YOU.

The Big-YOU has the ability to assign different vibrations or frequencies to match your experiences and desires. The Big-YOU understands the language of frequencies and vibrations and effortlessly orchestrates the necessary shifts to match your intentions.

Think of it as tuning a radio. You, the Human-YOU, decide that you want to listen to classic rock. You take the 'action' of asking the Big-YOU to adjust the frequency. The Big-YOU then seamlessly aligns your radio receiver with the corresponding frequency, bringing you your desired music.

Similarly, when you have a desire in life, the Big-YOU translates what you 'ask' for into the specific vibration needed to manifest it. This happens behind the scenes without you needing to understand the complex mechanisms involved.

So, instead of delving into the intricacies of frequency manipulation, focus on your desires, express them clearly to the Big-YOU, and trust that the process of aligning your vibration is already underway. If you are curious to learn more, simply ask the Big-YOU to reveal more information, and it will guide you towards a deeper understanding.

In summary, your role is to set intentions and express your desires while your Big-YOU handles the mechanics of vibration and frequency, translating what you 'ask' for into attracting the experiences and outcomes you seek from the universal database of your existence.

The Curated Outcome

(Your Human and Essence's Role)

By harmonising the Human-YOU and the Big-YOU, we attract our preferred outcome. The Human-YOU provides the impetus through action, while the Big-YOU guides us with its elevated frequency and vibration.

By embracing the roles of the Human-YOU and the Big-YOU and incorporating the Lucky Formula into our daily lives, we empower ourselves to consistently create a magnetic pull that draws our desired outcome towards us.

Focus, Belief and Emotion: Bringing It All Together

Imagine a life where you consistently attract your desired outcomes, where luck seems to be on your side. It is not magic but a powerful formula that taps into the interconnectedness of your inner and outer worlds.

Curated Outcome

Integrating the Lucky Formula in daily life:

- Focus + Belief: When we focus our attention and strongly believe in a desired outcome, we create an emotional trigger. This emotional energy acts as the catalyst for action.
- Action or Doing: This is the tangible manifestation of our intentions. It is the act of taking concrete steps towards our desired outcome, fuelled by the emotional energy generated by focused belief.
- Frequency and Vibration: Our thoughts, emotions, and actions emit distinct frequencies and vibrations. The Big-YOU constantly interacts with the universe and attracts experiences and opportunities that resonate with our dominant energetic signature.

When we approach life with an open mind and heart, embracing new possibilities and cultivating positive emotions about potential outcomes, we empower our higher selves to guide us towards the most fulfilling experiences. This Lucky

Formula involves surrendering our rigid plans and allowing serendipity to work its magic. Here are some instances:

- Booking a holiday: Instead of meticulously planning an itinerary, trust in the unknown and let spontaneous opportunities unfold. This openness may lead to unexpected adventures and encounters that enrich your experience.
- Other situations: The same principle applies to various life situations. Whether it is starting a new project or navigating a challenging relationship, maintaining an open mindset and a positive outlook can foster a harmonious connection with our higher selves.

Chapter 4
The Two Realms: Topics on Awareness

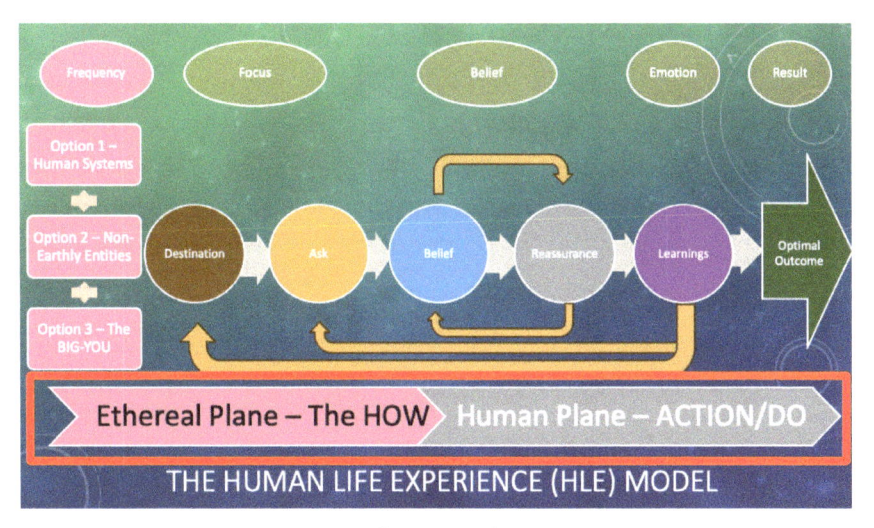

(Figure 4)

This chapter (Figure 4) explores the interaction between two distinct realms: the earthly realm inhabited by humans and the ethereal realm. It offers a straightforward interpretation of how these two interconnected planes influence each other.

This chapter is designed to stand on its own, allowing you to skip it if spirituality and the dynamics between these realms do not interest you. You can still read Chapters 1-3 and 5-6 and apply the accompanying method and formula to enrich your life. However, if this topic resonates with you, Chapter 4 provides additional insights that may enhance your overall understanding.

Chapter 4 delves into what I refer to as 'topics on awareness'—offering both a broad perspective and insights into the subtler, often unnoticed aspects of existence. It grapples with the timeless question of 'what is it all about'. These themes are derived from my experiences of connecting and collaborating with my Big-ME. While they may not encompass every aspect you might be curious about or provide exhaustive details, they serve a fundamental purpose for starting a discussion. This book aims to present various pathways to engage with the Big-YOU. Consider these topics as a starting point for your own journey of self-discovery and exploration alongside your Big-YOU.

Reading Chapter 4

The chapter encompasses over 100 topics related to awareness, which may initially feel lengthy and overwhelming due to its lack of organization, themes, or structure. This format is intentional; you, as the reader, have the freedom to navigate this chapter in whatever way suits you best:

- You can choose to read it sequentially, page by page.
- Alternatively, you might want to flip to a random page, akin to a lucky dip, and explore that particular topic.
- Another option is to skim through the topics, highlighting those themes and topics that pique your interest while skipping the rest.

The choice is entirely yours.

THE TWO YOUS

The Big-YOU inhabits the earthly plane through the Human-YOU, which is the human avatar within the earthly game. A form of tether joins the two together. Some have called it a silver cord, but whatever it is, it will attach the Big-You and the Human-You and help them sync with each other for the lifetime that you are both alive and playing the game. When you are playing the game, you are a single entity made up of the Human-YOU, the Big-YOU and a joint consciousness[3].

When you become aware and awakened, the purpose of this new 'life' is the harmonious collaboration between the Human and the Big-YOU and the new adventures both can experience within the confines of the earthly game. The Big-YOU still plays by earthly rules, such as gravity or that a human can only breathe oxygenated air to survive. The new collaboration is about the effective curation of both lives.

The Big-YOU is the player of the game—it chooses to enter this game, have a purpose and do and experience certain things during the game's lifetime. However, the veil of forgetfulness and the consent to play by earthly rules mean that it needs the Human-YOU as a vessel to experience all the senses of being within the game.

So, it is a mutually beneficial arrangement. Becoming aware of this and understanding the new arrangement between yourselves means that it is now a whole new adventure, a new experience, a new perspective and a new zone for curation. Your new awareness is unique to you. As you embark on this lifelong journey, use each realisation or understanding to fill your life with joy and peace.

---

3 Consciousness, at its simplest, is awareness of internal and external existence.

SCEPTICISM AND DISCERNMENT

Scepticism and a healthy dose of discernment ensure that you filter out what your conscious brain is telling you rather than what your heart or gut intuition, essentially, your Big-YOU is informing and guiding you to do. It is the Human-YOU using all its senses to know what it should do next.

We have heard of situations where someone has avoided a potentially lethal outcome because they had a bad feeling about it. Initially, they ignore it as they are sceptical. It feels like it is just nerves or silliness. But if the feeling is strong enough, they discern that they must act upon their feelings and will alter their plans. This is the Big-YOU guiding you on what to do next, but it may also be the prelude to a massive change in your life.

Thus, scepticism and discernment allow the Human-YOU to test and have reassurance in the process to build your trust, belief, and confidence in the Big-YOU. The Human-YOU routinely listens and acts on the Big-YOU's guidance, knowing that they have your human self's best interests at heart and that things will work out as they should, which allows for an exciting experience.

TIME: A SIMPLIFIED EXPLANATION

Time - An Earthly Concept

As a linear progression, dividing the past, present, and future, time is a human construct that aids our limited perception of reality. In essence, there is only an eternal present moment.

Just as a live streaming service simultaneously plays a multitude of channels, the present holds an infinite spectrum of events and experiences happening all at once. As observers, we have the ability to focus on or engage with specific moments, much like changing channels on the streaming service.

All of time is fundamentally interconnected and malleable, allowing us to explore and navigate them to shape our own unique journeys. When we access past lives, alternative presents or future realities, our human consciousness is presented with the most relevant and beneficial information for our growth and understanding in our current incarnation.

The Universal Records: A Database of Time

The concept of the past, present and future is like a universal database. Known to some as the Akashic Records, the Universal Records or Library of Life, it contains the entirety of our past and other lives, experiences, and the collective wisdom of the universe.

Similar to how data is stored and retrieved from a cloud-based system, so is our perceived experience of time.

The human mind acts as a processor and engages with this vast database. It selects focused information that it is interested in, processes it in the present, and uploads the results back to the Universal Records. These results encompass our feelings, emotions and the impact of our actions.

The Universal Records contain an infinite array of potential timelines, akin to a streaming service offering a multitude of programs. The Big-YOU has access to this boundless knowledge. It can revisit any moment in our timeline, like skipping through the different channels on a streaming service.

As we alter our intentions and focus, the past and future may shift accordingly. This curated timeline is fluid and adaptable. As the Human and Big-YOU collaborate, we can alter our future and, consequently, our past. The Universal Records readjust themselves, ensuring consistency between the past, present and future. Physical artifacts such as photos, videos and other storage media will also adjust to support the new past memory.

Breadcrumbs Showing Other Timelines

Occasionally, remnants of previous timelines emerge as breadcrumbs, such as the Mandela Effect, where memories of past events differ between individuals. The Mandela Effect refers to false memories shared by many people, such as the widespread belief that Nelson Mandela died in prison in the 1980s. These are intentional cues designed to indicate a shift in our timeline. They serve as progress reports, assisting us in understanding our evolving journey and encouraging us to question the nature of our existence.

I experienced this when I discovered an amazing truth about a persistent cough that I had for years, which was linked to a past lifetime. The revelation suggested that events from our past or other lifetimes can have a lasting impact on our present.

I was presented with a remarkable opportunity—to change the past timeline by accessing a different version that would no longer influence my current life. I chose to do so, and the result was that, over a period of time, my cough vanished.

This experience illuminated the interconnectedness of all our lifetimes. Each life exists simultaneously, often influencing one another through a ripple effect. For instance, the spirits responsible for my cough acted according to a pre-existing agreement between our collective essences. Their intervention served as a catalyst for my awakening, leading me to recognise the Big-Me, the totality of my being, across all lifetimes. Once I consciously acknowledged this connection, the need for the cough disappeared, fulfilling the agreement's purpose and releasing me from its influence.

This understanding of time empowers us. It reveals that we are not confined by the past or bound to the future or even by lifetimes. We possess the ability to shape our experiences by accessing different data points and choosing alternative realities. By acknowledging the Big-YOU and working with its guidance, we can create new and exciting pathways, unlocking the full potential of our journey.

ALONE BUT NOT LONELY

As individuals progress on their journey towards self-awareness, they often encounter a period of aloneness. This solitude arises as relationships dissolve and new connections are yet to materialise. While one may be alone, it is imperative to recognise that this phase does not equate to loneliness.

During this time of solitude, the individual sheds the limitations of their human persona and embarks on a profound exploration of their true essence and being. They recognise that their human form is merely a vessel for their boundless, non-physical self—the Big-YOU. The realisation brings a sense of connection to the vast and infinite ocean of souls.

This period of solitude signals the dawn of a new chapter, replete with unexplored territories and unforeseen opportunities. It is a time for renewal, self-rejuvenation, and the cultivation of a deeper understanding of one's purpose in the grand tapestry of life.

CONSTANT REASSURANCE

A yearning for constant reassurance that we are not out of our minds accompanies the journey of awakening. Designed to allow us to immerse ourselves in the sensory world, it arises from the veil of forgetfulness of the Big-YOU that shrouds our human experience. We may taste the rich chocolate, smell the intoxicating aroma of coffee and lose ourselves in the depths of human emotions, all while our Big-YOU, our spiritual essence, remains veiled.

This intentional separation creates a conflict between our human self and our awakened awareness. We may find ourselves questioning our newfound intuition, doubting the whispers of guidance from our spirits or the Big-YOU. This disbelief is an integral part of the earth game, a test of our trust and connection with our higher selves.

The solution? Embrace the need for reassurance. Engage in constant dialogue with your Big-YOU and your spirit guides, asking for validation and confirmation. They understand the human predicament, the struggle to integrate our awakened awareness within the confines of physical reality. They will readily provide the reassurance you seek, knowing it helps you navigate this challenging terrain.

As an individual who has experienced this journey, I often find myself pulled into the whirlwind of earthly matters, caught up in the daily dramas of family, work and global events. It is easy to fall back into old patterns of dealing with these challenges, forgetting the newfound connection with my Big-ME. However, I learned to recognise this pull and intentionally step back. I create space for myself, whether through a meditative walk or a quiet moment of reflection, and reconnect with my Big-ME. I ask for a sign, a reassurance that I am not losing my mind, that I am not alone in this journey. Invariably, the reassurance comes, reaffirming the bond between my human self and my spiritual essence.

This constant reassurance, this ongoing dialogue with our higher selves, is essential for navigating the veil between human experience and awakened awareness. It is a testament to the power of intention and the willingness to trust the guidance that lies within us all.

THE HUMAN-YOU: A VEHICLE FOR THE SOUL'S JOURNEY

The realisation that our physical self, the Human-YOU, is merely a vessel for a greater, eternal Big-YOU can be both profound and liberating. But what is the purpose of this human vessel? It is like owning a car. We want it to be reliable, efficient and able to take us where we want to go.

Similarly, the human vessel is designed to provide the Big-YOU with the opportunity to experience the richness of the earthly realm. The Big-YOU can immerse itself in the world through our seven senses, feeling joy, sorrow, beauty and pain.

But this journey is not random. The Big-YOU chooses the vessel, carefully selecting its initial programming—from our physical attributes, such as gender and location, to our personality traits, passions and even potential life circumstances. This initial programming ensures we are best suited to experience and complete the Big-YOU's pre-determined themes and purposes.

Shaped by our education, family, relationships and even the random events unfolding around us, layers of further programming are added throughout our lives. These experiences, however, are not arbitrary. The Big-YOU may have contracted with other souls before birth to engage in specific thematic interactions, perhaps a challenging marriage or a transformative friendship.

We are the ideal vessel chosen by the Big-YOU because we are the most suitable for fulfilling its specific purpose within the greater game of existence. With its complete understanding of all that exists, the Big-YOU makes no mistakes. It chose us because we are the best vehicle for its journey.

Therefore, let us embrace our role as vessels, collaborating with the Big-YOU to make this journey extraordinary. Our commitment to personal growth and the pursuit of meaningful experiences will not only enrich our own lives but also allow the Big-YOU to accomplish its grand purpose in this earthly realm.

THE POWER OF BELIEF: A PARKING SPACE STORY

The idea of curating your desires through belief is a powerful one, and the 'car parking method' is a popular example. You may have heard of it from the TV movie The Secret (2006), but it is a concept that goes beyond entertainment. It is the belief that whenever you are in a vehicle and are going to your destination, you will always get a parking space either outside or very close to where you want to be.

For years, I worked as a driver for a logistics company, traversing countless locations throughout the United Kingdom. During this time, I adopted the car parking method, believing that I would always find a convenient parking space. And it worked! In 99.9 percent of cases, I found a spot right where I wanted it.

Of course, there were times when the desired parking space wasn't available. That's where the concept of a 'bigger picture' comes into play. Perhaps the universe, or as some call it, the Big-YOU, had a different plan.

Maybe there was heavy traffic ahead, or another reason why finding a space right there would have been inconvenient.

The key is to trust the process, understanding that even when things don't go exactly as planned, there is a reason behind it. The Lucky Formula might be leading you to a better, even if unexpected, outcome. So, stay open to the possibilities and embrace the journey, knowing that even a missed parking space might be a blessing in disguise.

ASKING FOR CLARITY

The beauty of connecting with our higher selves or other spirits lies in its boundless freedom. Unlike structured religions or practices, there isn't a prescribed set of rules or rituals to follow. While respect, love and good intentions are essential, the specific form of communication is entirely up to you—because it is You!

This openness means that questions, even if they seem naive or unconventional, are always welcome. If you receive confusing guidance, do not hesitate to seek clarification. Remember, there are no stupid questions.

Even if your higher self sometimes finds your human limitations frustrating, it understands your unique perspective and is ultimately supportive. Embrace this open dialogue, and trust that your questions will lead you to a deeper understanding.

BEING SUPPORTED BY THE BIG-YOU

Does the Big-YOU always have the best intentions for the Human-YOU? The answer is unequivocally affirmative. However, the nature of the Big-YOU's intentions for the Human-YOU may not be immediately apparent.

The Big-YOU is an integral part of us and utilises the Human-YOU as an instrument to fulfil its goals and needs within this current incarnation. Possessing an omniscient perspective, the Big-YOU comprehends the broader circumstances and anticipates events. It experiences our sensations and emotions directly, including those that are unpleasant or distressing. While the Big-YOU may seek to shield the Human-YOU from negative experiences, it requires our attention and cooperation.

By allowing the Big-YOU to guide us, we access its wisdom and avoid unnecessary obstacles. This collaboration is mutually beneficial. It has been demonstrated that individuals learn more rapidly and effectively when motivated by positive reinforcement rather than punishment.

Challenging the Big-YOU's guidance is akin to rejecting its assistance, implying that the Human-YOU possesses superior knowledge. However, the Big-YOU, driven by unconditional love, respects the Human-YOU's free will, allowing you to make decisions and experience the consequences.

Therefore, we create a fulfilling existence by fostering a harmonious partnership with the Big-YOU. As our benevolent guardian, the Big-YOU prioritises our well-being, having chosen us as its vessel before incarnation. Through this collaboration, we can navigate life's challenges with greater ease and embrace its boundless possibilities.

UNPLUGGING FROM THE MATRIX OR THE EARTHLY GAME

The concept of unplugging from the Matrix evokes a powerful image of liberation, a break from the perceived constraints of reality. But what does it truly mean?

The idea is rooted in the understanding that we exist on multiple levels. We have the Big-YOU, the essence of our consciousness, which transcends the physical world. This Big-YOU experiences shows glimpses of its true nature through dreams, astral projections, and near-death experiences. These moments represent temporary escapes from the Matrix or the earthly realm, offering a taste of the boundless reality beyond the confines of our physical existence.

The Human-YOU, however, is inextricably woven into the fabric of the Matrix. We are the players in the game, our physical bodies and experiences forming the very foundation of the reality we perceive. When our human role is complete, the Human-YOU ceases to exist, and our energy disperses, contributing to the ever-evolving tapestry of the game.

Therefore, the desire to unplug from the Matrix requires careful consideration. Are we referring to the yearning of the Human-YOU for a different reality, a longing for freedom from the limitations of our physical form? Or is it the Big-YOU seeking to transcend the game entirely to awaken to a higher consciousness? Perhaps it is a call for a new partnership between the Human-YOU and the Big-YOU, a collaborative effort to create a more fulfilling and meaningful experience within the game.

Ultimately, the path to liberation lies in understanding our true, authentic nature, the interconnectedness of our being and the choices we make within the game. We can choose to play with awareness, seek deeper meaning and purpose and cultivate a connection with the divine reality that lies beyond the Matrix. While challenging, this journey offers the potential for profound growth and expansion of our knowledge, ultimately leading us closer to our own unique brand of liberation.

THE BIG-YOU

CURATING THE TAPESTRY OF YOUR LIFE

All versions of your life story exist storred in the Untiversal Daebase

Universal Database

Life's tapestry unfolds as a symphony of potential experiences, a tapestry woven from the threads of countless possible futures. The concept of curating your life entails the conscious selection and arrangement of these potential experiences, shaping the trajectory of your existence.

This universal database, also known as the Akashic Records, a vast repository of all conceivable events, holds within it every conceivable version of your life's journey, including the past, present and future. As the Human-YOU, you possess the innate ability to tap into this database, guided by the wisdom of the Big-YOU.

The Big-YOU operates on a grand scale, orchestrating events and experiences to nudge you towards your joint, desired destiny. You can align your intentions with the Big-YOU through the Lucky Formula described in Chapter 3.

While it may seem that you, as the Human-YOU, have the power to curate and manifest your life, this is not entirely true. Your role is to collaborate with the Big-YOU, entrusting it with the delicate task of guiding your path. By expressing your desires and intentions, you communicate with the Big-YOU, who then harnesses the power of the universal database to select and weave together the experiences that will lead you towards your aspired future. This can manifest in both the immediate present and the distant future as the Big-YOU works tirelessly to weave the tapestry of your life.

THE EARTHLY PLANE: A PLAYGROUND OF EXPERIENCE AND LEARNING

The earthly plane serves as a multifaceted realm where we engage in a profound interplay of gameplay and a transformative learning journey. It resembles a celestial holodeck, a three-dimensional hologram, granting us the freedom to explore, experience and evolve.

This cosmic playground is shaped by the collective experiences of countless beings, forming the tapestry of its ever-evolving storyline. Each essence and soul contributes their unique threads to the fabric, influencing its future direction. However, an underlying framework analogous to the hardware and software of a virtual environment provides a foundation for our experiences.

Upon entering this earthly realm, our Higher Selves, or Big-YOUs, agree to abide by certain rules, such as the laws of gravity. These parameters provide structure and constrain the boundaries of our gameplay. Yet, within this framework, we possess immense freedom to curate, explore and learn.

Our Big-YOUs, whether new to Earth or veterans of countless incarnations, choose their roles with a purpose. Each lifetime presents valuable lessons and opportunities for spiritual growth. Our experiences, both joyous and challenging, enrich the tapestry of our collective knowledge.

In one of my own other-life regressions, I witnessed the poignant existence of an elderly man imprisoned in a dungeon. My Higher Self explained that it had chosen this experience for the profound insights into the nature of suffering and resilience. Through this challenging journey, the spirit grew in empathy and understanding.

The earthly plane is thus both a vibrant playground and a sacred schoolroom. By embracing its lessons and immersing ourselves in its experiences, we evolve as beings of consciousness, contributing to the cosmic weaving that sustains us all.

This scenario may evoke a sense of insensitivity from a human standpoint. However, it is crucial to the question: whose life is it ultimately?

From the perspective of the Big-YOU, the life in question pertains to it and the experiences and lessons it desires. Therefore, from its viewpoint, the circumstances and trials endured by the human vessel in the dungeon are not inherently cruel or heartless. Rather, they serve as valuable catalysts for growth and learning.

My understanding, gleaned from my interactions with the Big-Me, is that a greater awareness of each other within this game leads to a more collaborative and less callous approach. This does not mean that difficult experiences, such as illness, loss or challenges, are automatically avoided. Instead, it suggests that these experiences may be designed with the understanding and consent of both the Human and the Big-YOU, as part of a shared, greater plan for growth.

THE VEIL OF FORGETFULNESS: A JOURNEY OF DISCOVERY

Veil Of Amnesia

The concept of a Big-YOU—a powerful, all-knowing entity—entering the earthly game, a realm of human experience, necessitates a crucial element, the veil of forgetfulness. This veil, a deliberate act of forgetting one's true nature, is essential for the very essence of the game itself.

Imagine knowing all the answers and experiencing every outcome before it unfolds. Such a reality would render the game meaningless, devoid of the thrill of discovery, the heartache of loss, the joy of triumph. Without the veil, the human experience would be devoid of the very emotions and sensations that give it meaning and purpose.

Therefore, in its infinite wisdom, the Big-YOU agrees to forget its origins, its vast knowledge and its omnipotent powers. It chooses to enter the game as a blank slate with a fresh perspective. This allows for an immersive experience, unhindered by prior knowledge, where every moment is a new revelation, a chance to learn, grow and truly feel.

The Big-YOU, however, never entirely abandons the Human-YOU. It acts as a silent guide, offering subtle hints and nudges through human senses, subtly steering the Human-YOU towards a path aligned with its 'mission', a purpose that was set before entering the game. This guidance, however, is never intrusive, never forces you and always respects the free will and choices of the Human-YOU.

The veil of forgetfulness, therefore, is not a barrier but a bridge. It allows for a profound journey of discovery, a rollercoaster of emotions and a profound connection with the human experience. Through this veil, this act of forgetting, the Big-YOU and the Human-YOU embark on a shared adventure, a quest for understanding and growth.

PATIENCE WITHOUT EXPECTATION

Patience, an essential trait for human experience, plays a pivotal role in our relationship with our higher selves. It allows us to navigate life with calm and trust, even in the face of unexpected challenges.

One such experience recently occurred as I drove my mother to the hospital. As I entered the car park, my usual expectation of finding a convenient parking space was unmet. Frustration bubbled within me, but I sensed an inner voice urging me to wait patiently and continue circling the car park.

My patience was rewarded after several minutes. An ideal parking spot emerged right by the hospital entrance, complete with a wheelchair-accessible area for my mother. It was as if the universe had conspired to meet my needs.

This experience embodies the power of patience. It invites us to surrender our immediate desires and allow the larger forces of life, the Big-YOU, to orchestrate a path that may not always be immediately apparent to our earthly selves. By trusting in the wisdom of our higher selves, we open ourselves to unexpected and often extraordinary outcomes.

Patience without expectations empowers us to do the following:

- Accept setbacks with grace: Instead of resisting obstacles, we can view them as catalysts for growth and learning.
- Stay present in the moment: By focusing on the immediate task, we can avoid becoming overwhelmed by future uncertainties and stop worrying.
- Create space for miracles: When we allow patience to guide us, we create room for the unexpected and the extraordinary to unfold.

Remember, patience is not passive resignation but an active and intentional choice. It requires us to believe that the universe is working in our favour and that all pieces of our lives will eventually fall into place. By embracing patience, we cultivate inner peace and open ourselves to the limitless possibilities that lie before us.

THE ILLUSION OF SCARCITY: MONEY, WEALTH AND THE GAME OF LIFE

The concept of money, a uniquely human invention, starkly contrasts with the abundance of the natural world. While all life on Earth, including humans, is provided for with the essential resources for survival—water, food and shelter— only humans have devised a system of exchange based on an artificial construct, that is, money. However, this system isn't merely a tool for trade. It is a game with its own set of rules and consequences designed to elevate the experience of life to another level. This elevation, however, manifests in both positive and negative ways.

The illusion of scarcity, deeply ingrained in our collective consciousness, tells us that money is limited in supply and is essential for survival. While it is true that our cultural conditioning, upbringing and environment shape our perceptions of money, this belief is ultimately a fabrication. Central banks, the creators of money, demonstrate money's limitless nature by constantly generating new currency.

Money, then, is akin to other forms of energy and matter, flowing freely and abundantly. It is our perception and our belief in the myth of scarcity that holds us captive to worry and struggle. We can choose to transcend this illusion and embrace a future in which money, wealth and support freely flow to us, liberating us from the anxieties of material security and allowing us to focus on living a life of purpose and fulfilment.

The Principle of Giving and Receiving

It is said that, according to the laws of the universe, the universe mirrors our thoughts and actions. Thus, giving out money acts as a catalyst for the flow of energy, fostering a reciprocal flow of wealth towards us. However, when we hoard money, we inadvertently halt this flow, hindering its availability to us.

While spending money can stimulate its circulation, a more profound approach lies in our thoughts and emotions surrounding money. If we harbour fears of scarcity or feel anxious about its acquisition, the universe aligns with those beliefs, resulting in an intermittent flow of money.

It is essential for us to recognise that money is an energy source akin to oxygen or electricity, readily available when we need and request it, particularly when we connect to our Big-SELVES.

Nature teaches us that other life forms are provided for even without money. This begs the question, why not apply this principle to ourselves as adults? The premise is that the Big-YOU will always care for us, providing us with the means to thrive in unexpected ways. We may receive financial assistance from unconventional sources, discover new earning opportunities, encounter unexpected generosity or experience support from those around us.

It is crucial to emphasise that while giving is paramount, it need not always involve monetary contributions. Any act of sharing oneself, such as time, love, kindness, service or assistance, contributes to the flow of energy.

By embracing the principle of giving, we cultivate trust that the Big YOU will always provide for us, opening ourselves to limitless abundance in all its manifestations as set out under the laws of the universe.

UNDERSTANDING PERSPECTIVE IN THE JOURNEY OF AWARENESS

Perspective And Perception

As we become aware of our true selves, recognising the concept of perspective becomes crucial for navigating the earthly realm. It allows us to comprehend that all viewpoints hold value and that we are essentially discussing the same fundamental truths from different vantage points.

No single entity, belief or organisation possesses an absolute answer to life's complexities. Each perspective contributes a piece to the puzzle, and it is our responsibility as earthly beings to assemble these fragments.

In collaboration with the Big-YOU, our conscious selves have the task of organising these pieces of the puzzle into a coherent picture tailored to our individual understanding. While the complete picture may not reveal itself until the journey's end, we will receive the most pertinent portions when their impact and relevance are most profound.

Our Big-YOU attracts and curates knowledge and information that serves our growth on the earthly plane. This endeavour is deeply personal, resulting in a unique perspective for each individual. While all perspectives are valid, they ultimately converge on the same underlying truths.

By embracing this understanding of perspective, we recognise the interconnectedness of all knowledge and the importance of respecting diverse viewpoints. As we navigate our journey of awakening, we can strive to gather insights from multiple sources, expand our understanding and contribute meaningfully to the collective tapestry of human consciousness.

YOUR INTUITIVE SAT-NAV: THE BIG-YOU

Prior to its incarnation in the earthly game, the higher self or Big-YOU, determines its objectives and the optimal human form to inhabit in order to achieve them. The Big-YOU has a comprehensive understanding of the assigned human's life path and all potential variations and timelines.

On the other hand, the Human-You has genetic and personality traits that shape their skills and challenges. These traits may include strengths in areas, such as math, creativity or athletics, as well as limitations such as poor eyesight or mental health disorders. The combination of abilities and obstacles enables the Big-YOU to have a unique experience and growth opportunities in each lifetime.

The Big-YOU remains in the spiritual realm, while a portion of its consciousness merges with the human form. This can be compared to a video game player who is simultaneously in their physical space and immersed in the game through their headset. However, upon entering the physical realm, the higher self may experience forgetfulness of its mission.

The Big-YOU has specific goals it aims to accomplish within the human experience, which are represented as anchor points or sensory events. With the assistance of spirit guides and other ethereal beings, the Big-YOU strives to achieve these objectives before departing from the physical earthly world.

The Human-YOU possesses free will and can act independently within the earthly realm without direct intervention from the Big-YOU. This design allows the Big-YOU to have a unique and immersive experience.

The Big-YOU and its helpers will subtly influence the Human-YOU through the seven senses, encouraging a return to the intended path. However, if the Human-YOU refuses to listen, the guidance may become stronger, potentially resulting in physical discomfort or illness. These experiences serve as signals for the Human-You to stop, reconsider and realign with the original plan.

It is not necessary for the Big-YOU to accomplish all its goals in a single lifetime as it has infinite opportunities to do so. Nonetheless, it will attempt to achieve as many as possible. Ultimately, the Human-YOU has the freedom to explore any path, and the Big-YOU will not object as all experiences hold value, interest and joy.

A more desirable approach is for the Human-YOU to cooperate with the Big-YOU as it serves as an intuitive guide and is knowledgeable about the optimal path for a rewarding life. The purpose of the human experience is to cultivate the best possible working relationship between the Human-YOU and the Big-YOU, enabling collaboration and creating a remarkable life for both entities.

THE HUMAN-YOU AND THE LIMITS OF CHANGE

The human journey is a constant interplay between acceptance and change where the limits of our potential remain a dynamic and evolving notion.

The ability of a human to significantly alter the timeline they are on is a complex issue. The Big-YOU, or the entity responsible for choosing the human's inherent traits, endows them with certain hardware and software, such as athletic ability, family orientation or physical disability. These innate traits, along with external programming from sources, such as parents, school, culture and religion, shape the human's belief system and determine their perceived potential for achievement.

I refer to this concept as the 'life potential funnel mechanism'. With a set of predetermined traits and beliefs, a human's future is likely to follow a predictable path. It is reasonable to assume that in the immediate future, a human's life will be 80 percent similar to its current state. This percentage decreases as the timeline extends, with a 60 percent likelihood of similarity in five years, 40 percent in 20 years, and potentially 20 percent in 50 years. The further into the human's future, the more unpredictable their path becomes.

Changing significant aspects of the human, such as transitioning from being a doctor to an astrophysicist, is possible but would require a substantial amount of time, potentially decades. The success of such a transformation would depend on the human's belief system, the will of the Big-YOU, and the constraints of their innate and externally imposed programming. While small changes may be easy to implement, more radical shifts are likely to be met with resistance.

Can we accelerate radical change in our lives? The answer lies in recognising the transformative power of the Big-YOU. It possesses an expansive consciousness that encompasses all possible timelines and potential outcomes. When our conscious self, the Human-YOU veers off course, the Big-YOU intervenes to steer us back towards our desired path. Usually, this is via nudges and whispers from your ethereal guides.

With certain situations such as when the Human-YOU is doing their own thing and it is decided by your guides that a major intervention is needed, such as near-death experiences or life-altering accidents, which can serve as life altering wake-up calls from the ethereal realm.

These events prompt the Human and Big-YOU within the game to re-evaluate its life path and make a new course of action. This is like sports, where a time-out or timeout is a halt in the game play. This allows the coaches (the ethereal Big-YOU, your guides, deity, spirits, souls family) to communicate with the earthly-YOU e.g., to determine strategy or inspire morale, as well as to stop the game clock for a period of reflection, instruction and perspective.

According to the concept of the Big-YOU and timelines presented in this book, The Big-YOU is the puppeteer and performs the mechanics of selecting potential past, present and future timelines from the universal database or records. If you, the Human-YOU, yearn for a significant transformation, you can seek guidance from the Big-YOU, who will provide a path towards realising this change, if it aligns with its master plan. There is testimony and evidence of humans actively changing their timelines from being a professional chef to being able to speak foreign languages to knowing how to play a new musical instrument.

Therefore, it is possible for you to enhance and modify your life to a certain extent with the approval of the Big-YOU. Your Human-YOU was specifically designed to accomplish certain duties and missions planned by the Big-YOU. By cooperating with the Big-YOU throughout your life, you are more likely to have the best possible human experience. Therefore, to have a rewarding lifetime, it is recommended that you work in harmony with the Big-YOU and understand its intentions and aspirations.

LIVING YOUR TRUE AUTHENTIC LIFE

It is hard and challenging to carry on with your life on the earthly plane when both of you become aware of each other, that is, awakened. What is the point of it all? The simple answer is, of course, it is what the Big-YOU is here to do, and they want and desire to play the game to its full advantage.

The Human-YOU may not want to carry on doing the human job that you were doing before you became aware, as it may seem banal and a waste of time, but the Human-YOU needs to understand that having a job pays money, and you are still on the same version timeline as you were before you became aware.

Carry on doing the mundane essential things to survive in your life and try to do the things that give you the most pleasure in life. It requires action from your human self. So, it takes time to start listening to the Big-YOU about how to change the version of your life to something both of you prefer and which you want to do.

Listen to what the Big-YOU wants to try and achieve in this lifetime and collaborate with it. This will usually be an innate interest or passion you have from birth. Part of the earthly experience and journey is the discovery of this passion. Try out many things until you realise that what you are doing is what you love. It may not be a lifelong passion, but it could exist for just a short time. This could be many different things, such as writing, teaching, acting, doing something creative, entrepreneurial, caring, scientific, exploratory or project management.

The major theme of my Big-ME is helping others and understanding worthiness in all its aspects. My innate interests include learning about new places and new things, transmitting knowledge to others and small projects and adventures with a defined start, middle and end. I have been a diplomat, business owner, lecturer, project manager, business consultant, writer and speaker. The careers that I've had have incorporated all the above innate interests.

There were times when I strayed off the path of my authentic self because I needed a job, or it was a job I thought I should be doing due to peer or self-pressure. Guess what, I hated it, I was dreadful at it and ultimately left that job or was asked to move on. These jobs included being an accountant, in the army, a salesman and a teacher. In some cases, the Big-ME had to force me to change jobs because I did not want to move on or was scared to move on. The Big-ME gave me nudges and whispers to take action and move on, but as I was stubborn and thought I knew best, the Big-ME created a situation where I was made redundant or made the job so unpleasant that I left.

Ultimately, if you are doing what you love, you are doing what the Big-YOU wants to do, and it will make the path easier and more rewarding for you both. It knows the big picture and the exciting life avenues both of you can experience and explore. So, be as authentic to your innate self as possible, and you will thrive in this lifetime.

THE ARCHITECTS OF EARTHLY DESTINY

Much like a video game, life on Earth unfolds within a predetermined framework. We inherit a world already teeming with life, shaped by the natural processes that have been set in motion for eons—the oceans, the land, the vegetation and the intricate tapestry of other life forms. This provides the backdrop, the hardware and the software of our earthly experience.

But it is our collective souls playing in the earthly game, with the assistance of our spiritual guides and other angelic beings, who ultimately determine the storyline, shaping the rules of the game itself.

Through our thoughts, intentions and actions, and thus the Big-YOU's, we contribute to the unfolding narrative at various levels—personal, local, regional, global and universal.

When a collective desire for change emerges, it manifests as a powerful force, subtly altering the course of events. A shared vision for the future can manifest as new storylines or events that ripple through society, impacting the game at all levels. The recent global pandemic of 2019-21 serves as a stark example of how a shift in the collective consciousness can dramatically alter the rules of the game.

Therefore, we are not merely passive participants in this grand game of life. We are the architects of our reality, with the power to influence its direction and outcome. The choices we make, individually and collectively, shape the rules, guide the storylines and ultimately determine the future of our planet and ourselves.

NAVIGATING THE MULTIVERSE: SHIFTING VERSIONS AND TIMELINES

The idea of altering our versions or timelines might seem like science fiction, but the concept is gaining traction in metaphysical circles. The truth is all of us have the potential to shift our realities, and we do so on a moment-by-moment basis.

One powerful approach is through the Lucky Formula discussed in Chapter Three. It involves aligning ourselves with our Big-YOU and our true desires. By listening deeply to our inner wisdom and embracing the aspirations of our soul, we tap into a powerful force. This force, the Big-YOU, is the essence of our being, working behind the scenes to guide us towards our desired version of reality.

The key is unwavering belief—a firm conviction that we are indeed moving towards our desired timeline, allowing the Big-YOU to orchestrate the necessary changes.

While different individuals may prefer different methods and modalities to connect to the Divine, the ultimate outcome remains the same—a connection to our spiritual core. By accessing this inner wisdom, we empower ourselves to navigate the multiverse and shift realities, shaping our own destinies in the process.

ARE YOU IN AN ABUSIVE RELATIONSHIP WITH THE OUTSIDE WORLD?

Are you in an abusive relationship with the outside world?

What do I mean by this? We often feel bombarded by the outside world—news cycles, social media trends and societal expectations. It can feel like we are in constant struggle, reacting to the demands and pressures around us. What if we shifted this perspective? What if we understood that our lives are not solely defined by external forces but by our own internal choices and desires?

Imagine your life as a unique journey, a personal adventure for the growth and evolution of your soul. As a physical being and as your core essence, you are the central character in this story. Every experience, both good and bad, contributes to your growth and understanding.

With its endless array of possibilities and stimuli, the outside world becomes a buffet of potential experiences. You get to choose what resonates with you, what you want to explore and what you want to learn from. Think of it as a vast library of books—some captivating, some dull, some inspiring, some challenging. You get to pick what you want to read, and you don't have to read every single book on the shelf.

The key lies in recognising that you have the power to choose. You can choose to be influenced by external pressures, or you can choose to focus on your internal compass, on your own desires and aspirations. You can choose to be a passive observer, or you can choose to be an active participant in shaping your own life.

This doesn't mean ignoring external realities, but it does mean reclaiming your agency. It is about choosing to be in control of your emotions, your thoughts and your actions. It is about recognising that you are not a victim of circumstance but an active creator of your own experience.

So, instead of feeling like you are in an abusive relationship with the outside world, consider embracing the power within. You are the author of your own story, and you have the freedom to choose the direction you take. Choose to be empowered, choose to be in control, choose to live a life that is authentically you.

THE BIG-YOU

ALTERNATIVE REALITIES: HOW WE PERCEIVE THEM

The idea is that the Human-YOU has the free will to decide what you will focus on and, thus, the reality you will experience. All versions and realities exist, and consciously or unconsciously, we—the Human and the Big-YOU—select the timeline we wish to explore. We bring in or attract into ourselves all information from the outside to experience both past and future experiences.

This means that when you are living and curating your life and experiencing different things, you are in control of what you sense, perceive and experience.

The interesting aspect of alternative realities is when you have an input from the outside, you can do one of the following:

- Either observe it and decide that it is not your preference and move on.
- Or lock into it by using the Lucky Formula and explore it further.

On a larger scale, this is where a 'wow' moment occurs. When you interact with other people or inputs, you are not interacting with them. They are interacting with you, and their version of reality is presented to you, for example, version A, version M or version F. If the version you are experiencing and being presented with isn't your preference, you can ignore it and let it pass. Wait, and another version of them will be presented to you.

So, if something isn't your preference, if you ignore it, allow it to change and wish it to be changed, it will become an alternative version of reality because you have that power.

In a past instance, I met a new friend, and we got on very well. Something happened a few months later, and they ghosted me and weren't very happy to see or be in contact with me. But miraculously, a couple of years later, they came back into my life, and we have become best of friends. So, the question is—which version of that person was I experiencing? Was I seeing the version that I wanted or needed to see and experience at those junctures in my life?

Taking this even wider on a more humanistic scale. All of us have the free will to decide whether we want to focus and lock in any event or issue and its version. Let us say, you are a 'people pleaser' or a 'fixer'. You perceive that someone in your life or focus needs help, and you attempt to fix them. You have locked into their version, where they have a specific issue, and you will explore it further. However, if you had waited and allowed them to change the reality that is being presented to you, a different version of them would have come into your life that would not require fixing.

This is quite powerful and can be expanded further. If you focus on a thing, you don't like and try to change it, for example, you participate in demonstrations, you have locked into that version, and that version will be played out. Ultimately, you have curated the negativity in your life. If you had decided to ignore it, remain neutral and let it pass, maybe a new version would occur, which you would have in your life.

Let us take this even more global. If all humans come together in a negative way, they lock in to and focus on a bad scenario, an event that isn't their preference, such as war, plays out in all our consciousnesses and experiences. Going back to the concept of non-interference, on the other hand, if you didn't interfere but simply observed it and said, "Well, that's not my preference. It is my existence, my gameplay. I want to live in a peaceful world," that too plays out.

We have proof that this happens all the time. Some people live in war zones and have a relatively peaceful existence unaffected by war, while others are battered and affected by the war. The Big-YOU chooses which one it wishes to experience. In collaboration, the Human-YOU and the Big-YOU can decide upon the type of war experience to explore.

If all humans wanted a more positive, peaceful world, guess what! A peaceful world would emerge and exist. How do we know this can happen? Look at groups of people when they gather—whether it is religious or music venues and concerts or a variety of situations where people come together in a harmonious, celebratory, positive way, amazing things happen. This is proven time and time again.

So, the ultimate wow moment for the Human-ME in collaboration with the Big-ME was the realisation that I was curating the version of reality being presented to me to choose from and explore further.

SYMBIOTIC RELATIONSHIP

The Big-YOU decided that it wanted the Human-YOU with all your attributes, personality traits, flaws and characteristics. You are the best version for what the Big-YOU wants to achieve in its lifetime. Why? Because it has the sat nav map of all your lives and your potential life path. It does the 'How'. It knows every possible outcome of your existence, and it chose you to do its work on the earthly plane.

Your life paths are aligned at birth but will usually diverge as the Human-YOU grows up because you have free will to do as you want in the game. You also don't have the master plan of the Big YOU, and you are interacting with and being guided by others in the game. The Big-YOU will do its best to bring you back into alignment by using your instinct and senses and using the carrot and stick method to help with your realignment.

The sense of non-alignment will be negative, a hollow feeling, sadness, pain, frustration, anger, disappointment, self-loathing, pessimism, a feeling of eternity, discomfort, dread, distractedness, a feeling that something's wrong, doubt and emptiness.

Conversely, alignment gives a sense of completeness, joy, happiness, timelessness, positivity, optimism, luck, passion, calmness, hope, peacefulness, focus and a feeling of attractiveness and purpose.

So, be thankful and grateful. Rest assured that the Big-YOU has the best and the highest intentions for you both. Therefore, you should have the best intentions for the Big-YOU. If you can create a loving working relationship and symbiotic connection with each other, you will have an amazing life together. Always realise that your Big-YOU loves and cares for you deeply.

When you work together, you will no longer feel lost or empty. Those feelings only emerge when you are separated from each other and the Human-YOU 'goes it alone'.

The Big-YOU loves you enough to let you go because you were designed to do that if you wanted. However, the Big-YOU and your guides will send loving nudges to bring you back home to the life path. From the perspective of the Big-YOU, even if the Human-YOU goes its own way, it is still a valid adventure and experience.

NPCS: NON-PLAYER CHARACTERS

A viewpoint exists that as the Human-YOU plays in this game of life, everyone around you is just energy without any soul or essence in them, that they are soulless avatars in the background.

I have a more nuanced viewpoint of all the people around me. I believe that all life forms, including the Earth, have their own essence or soul in them. It depends upon the degree of the Essence focus and, thus, the lifetime versions.

What do I mean by this? To illustrate the point, the human being that I am, has an essence in it. It is playing a game to learn things, experience them and have emotions for the lifetime of the human version of me. As time goes by, the Human-ME makes choices, and a new version or timeline is created after each choice. However, the one that the Human-YOU is conscious of is the timeline that the Big-YOU is focusing on.

All other versions and timelines exist and have a part of your essence inhabiting and experiencing them. However, the timeline that is relevant to both your Human-YOU and the Big-YOU is the one focused on at the time. You could call it the primary version timeline.

So, how does this relate to NPCs, the non-player characters? Where the Human-YOU interacts with another soul—human or otherwise—if that soul is in the same timeline version as yours, both will be at 100 percent focus. However, if it is a soul that you don't interact with or share your timeline with, then the other soul may be in another timeline they are focused on. So, you would have a Soul that is at, say, 40 percent focus. You may see another Soul on TV, which is only at one percent focus for your life. They are in the background of your life to 'tell' the story, but they don't need to be at full focus in your life as they have their own versions of life and timelines to live.

So, as you interact with other humans and objects, their essence focus will change, as will yours towards theirs, depending on the interaction you need to have with each other. If both are to learn something from each other, there needs to be full attention and focus.

If only one learns from the other, it can be partial. It can be very minimal if there is no need for learning on either side, and they are just passing by.

RITUALS: A PATH TO MANIFESTATION

In the realm of manifestation, the 3.5.1 Method outlined in Chapter Two presents three potential options for connecting with the spirit. While all options have equal value, the choice ultimately depends on an individual's preference. Rituals come under the human viewpoint option.

Rituals encompass human practices, symbolism and objects with a deep human belief in their ability to produce desired outcomes. These may include meditation, prayer, affirmations, tarot cards, crystals, mantras, charms, spells and cherished keepsakes.

The key to unlocking the power of rituals lies in unwavering belief. This belief forms an integral component of the Lucky Formula described earlier. Individuals can cultivate their desired version of life by selecting rituals that resonate with their preferences and engaging in them with enthusiasm.

AWARENESS AND THE JOURNEY TO KNOWLEDGE

Other Teachers And Future Learnings

As individuals embark on a journey of self-discovery, they experience a heightened desire to seek knowledge from diverse sources. However, it is crucial to approach this pursuit with discernment and an open mind.

No single source holds the ultimate answer. We must engage with information actively, questioning, comparing and resonating with what feels authentic. Blindly following any one source, even this text, would limit our understanding.

Remember, this journey of learning is not solely for the Human-YOU, but also for the Big-YOU, the vast consciousness within us. In a sense, we are avatars playing this earthly game, and the Big-YOU guides our path, seeking experiences and knowledge that enrich its own understanding.

Drawn to us like magnets, the teachers and gurus we encounter along the way emerge when we are ready. We need not actively seek them out. The universe orchestrates perfect timing. Trust in the Big-YOU, knowing that exactly the right information will arrive at precisely the moment we need it. Patience is key. As one source of knowledge is assimilated, the journey progresses, leading to the discovery of new teachers and informational avenues.

Trust that the Big-YOU will provide the necessary knowledge at the appropriate pace, ensuring your optimal growth and the fulfilment of your collective purpose. Embrace the wisdom of the collective, approaching it with an open mind and a willingness to learn from diverse sources.

GLOBAL TRANSMITTERS: A NEW ERA OF CONSCIOUSNESS

Your Voice Is Your Transmitter For Change

The concept of global transmitters refers to individuals who have become aware of a higher understanding of their existence. This awakening often involves a profound realisation of the spiritual realm and the interconnectedness of all beings. These awakened individuals recognise that their earthly experience is a journey of growth, exploration and fun, played out through the avatar of their human form. This realisation fundamentally shifts their perspective and creates a new zone of existence within the earthly game.

This new zone, characterised by heightened awareness and spiritual understanding, holds immense potential for positive change. However, its emergence faces a challenge—the presence of unawakened individuals who may inadvertently hinder its growth.

Recognising this potential conflict, the spiritual realm, including both those experiencing the earthly game and those invested in Earth's development, have devised a strategy—mass awakening. The belief is that millions of humans transmitting this new information and embracing this awakened state will have a profound impact on the earthly game. This influx of conscious energy will not only ensure the thriving and expansion of this new zone but also gradually diminish the power and influence of outdated, negativity-driven zones.

This approach allows for the continued existence of older, less enlightened zones while simultaneously creating space for a new, more conscious reality to flourish. This dynamic creates a tapestry of diverse experiences where individuals can choose their path based on their individual levels of awareness and growth.

POST-DEATH PROCESS: A TRANSITION OUT OF HERE

Upon transitioning out of human life, the essence known as the Big-YOU returns to the cosmic origin, the big ocean or the source, the spiritual realm. Various factors influence the way this transition occurs, including the following:

1. Beliefs and Cultural Heritage:
    - Individuals who hold religious beliefs may perceive a deity or religious figure, such as Jesus Christ, Buddha, or Muhammad, as a reference point for their return.
    - Non-religious individuals may encounter deceased loved ones or other spiritual guides who provide guidance and support during the transition.
2. Pre-Death Agreements:
    - Prior to death, the Big-YOU collaborates with other spiritual entities to establish a mutually agreed-upon reference point for the transition.
    - This reference point serves as a familiar anchor for the Big-YOU's return.

Analogy of Waking from Anaesthesia:

- The experience of transitioning back to the source or the ethereal plane has been likened to waking up from surgery under general anaesthesia.
- Upon awakening, the Big-YOU may initially feel disoriented and confused.
- The presence of comforting figures, such as loved ones or spiritual guides, provides reassurance and support during this transition.

In essence, the Big-YOU's transition back to the source is guided by a combination of individual beliefs, cultural influences and pre-determined agreements. By establishing a reference point, the Big-YOU ensures a smooth and supported transition from human life to the boundless realm of spirit.

THE ART OF CURATING EXISTENCE: A SYMPHONY OF BIG-YOU AND HUMAN-YOU

You Have The Power Of Selection And Engagement

The question of whether we create or curate our existence is a fascinating one. While the concept of creation might imply bringing something into being from nothing, I propose that we are more akin to curators, carefully selecting and shaping the experiences we desire.

This perspective stems from the idea that everything, every possibility, already exists within a vast, universal database. The Big-YOU, a representation of our higher self, acts as the curator, drawing upon this infinite library of experiences. The Human-YOU, our individual consciousness, provides the emotional fuel and focused belief that guides the Big-YOU's selection.

The Human-YOU's desires, fears and aspirations all play a role in determining the potential paths the Big-YOU chooses to manifest. It is as if we are navigating a grand library, with each book representing a possible future. The intensity of our desires, the clarity of our beliefs, and the strength of our emotions directly influence which books we ultimately select.

Therefore, rather than create our reality from scratch, we refine and curate it, choosing from a pre-existing tapestry of possibilities. This realisation empowers us to become active participants in shaping our own lives. We can consciously choose to focus on positive emotions and strengthen our beliefs in a positive outcome, thus creating a more desirable and fulfilling future.

Let us then embrace our role as curators, actively selecting and shaping the world we wish to experience. By cultivating positive emotions, aligning our beliefs with our desires and focusing on the best possible outcomes, we can co-create a life that reflects our highest aspirations and contributes to the betterment of the world around us.

THEMES AND EXPERIENCES FOR THE BIG-YOU

The Big-YOU comes down to play the earthly game to explore themes and experiences throughout that lifetime. The Human-YOU can radically change what it is doing monthly, yearly or in decades. The Big-YOU will want to hit major milestones, explore certain themes and learn through sensory experiences during this lifetime.

For instance, I have done various things since leaving school. I joined the military in the reserve army. I became a diplomat and travelled the world, ran my own business for a few years and worked in corporate jobs. Now I am writing a book. I never would have thought I could or should be writing a book because I am dyslexic. If you asked me a couple of years ago, I would have said it was madness. But the Big-ME decided it wanted me to transmit some information to the human world. So, they gave me the means and tools to write such a book.

What this shows is that the Human-YOU can change what it is doing all the time. These jobs I undertook have no correlation to one another, but they do share a similar theme—to help and hopefully improve other humans' lives. It has been one big adventure, and when I was a diplomat, I unconsciously went with the flow as I had not become aware at the time. I let the Big-ME do the 'How' of my life. What an amazing trip I've had!

EMBRACING THE JOURNEY: FREE WILL AND THE HUMAN EXPERIENCE

The human experience is a remarkable adventure, a sensory journey unlike any other. It is a unique opportunity for the Big-YOU to fully immerse itself in the earthly plane. Before it arrives, the soul creates a blueprint, a map of sorts, outlining its intentions and aspirations for this life.

However, entering the human form brings with it the gift of free will. This means the Human-YOU has the power to choose, to navigate its own path, making both good and bad choices. These choices, however, aren't simply random acts. Every decision and every action is a piece of the intricate tapestry woven by the soul's journey.

The earthly plane is a playground, a canvas upon which the soul can explore its potential, learn from its experiences, and ultimately grow. The human's freedom to choose, even if it leads to detours and unexpected turns, is an inherent part of this adventure. The Big-YOU understands this. It recognises that the human's free will is a crucial ingredient in the recipe for a rich, complex and ultimately fulfilling journey.

INSHALLAH, OJALÁ, AMEN

Expressions like Inshallah, Ojalá and Amen embody the notion of divine providence, conveying the sentiment 'if God wills it' or 'hopefully' or 'so be it'. They could be turned into the concept 'if your essence or Big-YOU wills it'.

Ultimately, our lives are a manifestation of the gameplay of our Big-YOU. If an event is aligned with its plan, it will facilitate its occurrence. By embracing this belief, we can delegate the 'How' to the divine and focus on our human actions.

This relinquishment of responsibility empowers us to live in the present, performing our designated roles with intention. By listening to and acting upon the guidance of our Big-YOU, we surrender the burden of deciding between different life paths. We acknowledge that a higher power is weaving the grand tapestry of our destiny.

Therefore, phrases like Inshallah and Amen serve as a reminder to embrace the unknown and accept the guiding hand of the Big-YOU. They encourage us to let go of worries and trust that our essence will manifest its desires through our actions. By embracing this perspective, we cultivate serenity and live with purpose, knowing that our Big-YOU is ultimately in control.

THE DOUBLE-EDGED SWORD OF OUTSIDE INFORMATION

The world bombards us with information—news articles, social media feeds, conversations with friends and even the gentle hum of our surroundings. This constant stream of outside inputs acts both as a catalyst for growth and a potential path to distraction.

On the one hand, external information fuels our learning and development. It exposes us to new ideas, perspectives and experiences, expanding our horizons and shaping our understanding of the world. It is through this constant intake that we grow intellectually, emotionally and even spiritually.

However, the sheer volume of information can be overwhelming. We risk becoming consumed by external narratives, losing ourselves in the rabbit holes of endless news cycles, social media trends or even others' opinions. The abundance of information can potentially trigger hyperfocus or obsessive behaviours. When we become overly invested in specific pieces of information, we may neglect other aspects of our lives. Additionally, external inputs can distract us from our intended goals and priorities. This can lead to a disconnect from our inner compass and feeling pulled in a million directions, often against our will.

Fortunately, we possess the tools to navigate this informational overload. One strategy is to cultivate internal awareness—listening to our Big-YOU, the voice within that whispers our true desires and instincts. Does this information feel aligned with our values and goals? Does it resonate with us on a deeper level? Trusting this inner guidance helps us discern what truly matters and what we can safely let go of.

Furthermore, we can practice selective attention. Just as we curate our message inboxes, choosing what to read and what to delete, we can apply the same principle to our lives. We can prioritise information that aligns with our authentic goals and values while consciously minimising exposure to distractions.

    The key lies in finding the balance. We must acknowledge the power of external information while embracing the responsibility to curate our own experience. By listening to our inner voice and making conscious choices about where we direct our attention, we can harness the benefits of external inputs while protecting ourselves from their potential pitfalls.

TRUSTING AND BELIEVING IN THE FLOW

Go With The Flow

Here's a nice analogy of what I mean by trusting and believing in the flow. Imagine a river flowing downstream, representing your lifetime. The Human-YOU is a sailing boat, and the Big-YOU is the wind.

The boat starts at a tributary upstream and starts to flow downstream with the added push from the wind. The boat can explore and has the free will to move anywhere on the river to visit its banks, islands, whirlpools or tributaries. The general flow is for the river and wind to push the boat downstream. But on occasion, the wind can be harnessed to help the boat move around obstacles or move quicker than the current flow of the water.

If, however, the boat decides to reverse course or go against the wind, it can do so, but the journey will be much harder and slower. It may even stop moving and start getting battered by other things in the river, such as rocks, fallen trees or other debris, which continue to flow downstream.

So, stop controlling your life, going against the flow and the wind and doing the 'How' to navigate the river. It is not your job—that is the role of the Big-YOU.

Everything in life has a reason or meaning to it—as a human, it is fun to figure it out, but it may just be to give the Big-YOU an experience or some light relief.

Here is an example. On my last dog walk, I allowed Maximus, my dog, to go where he wanted to walk, and we ended up going on a five-mile walk to a new part of the area. It was a wonderful adventure with beautiful scenery and perfect blue skies, all because I trusted and went with the flow. I did not try to control the walk. I let life take its course and follow the flow of the river.

THEORETICAL VERSUS PRACTICAL: A JOURNEY OF EXPANSION

There is often a distinction between theoretical and practical understanding in the realm of human knowledge. Theoretical understanding involves the acquisition of knowledge through books, lectures and other abstract sources. Practical understanding, on the other hand, requires direct experience and engagement with the subject matter.

This distinction holds true for the journey of our higher selves on the earthly plane. The Big-YOU comes to Earth to acquire new knowledge and expand its consciousness. Earth is considered a University of Learning where souls can progress and grow at a rapid pace.

The comparison of theoretical and practical knowledge highlights the importance of sensory and emotional experiences in facilitating deep understanding. Reading about a concept or idea is not the same as experiencing it firsthand. When one encounters something directly, we engage all our human senses and emotions, creating a more profound and transformative experience.

This is precisely what the Big-YOU seeks when it comes to Earth. It desires to feel and experience life in all its aspects, both joys and challenges. Through these experiences, it gains practical wisdom that cannot be obtained in any other realm.

Through the earthly game, it seeks to embody and feel the complexities of physicality, emotions and relationships. By doing so, it acquires invaluable knowledge and wisdom, which it can share with the collective source consciousness. This knowledge ultimately enriches the universal database, contributing to the growth and expansion of the entire cosmos.

THE POWER OF ACTION: FROM THOUGHT TO REALITY

Action is the bridge between thought and reality. It is the tangible expression of our intentions, the physical step we take to transform an idea into something concrete. Unlike mere thoughts or words, action carries weight. It is the doing, the execution, the actual movement that brings change.

Consider the spectrum of action from the simple act of blinking to the complex choreography of a dance, from the stillness of deep sleep to the exhilarating surge of a run. All these are actions, each a choice we make to interact with the world around us.

Our Big-YOU, our GPS sat nav, can only provide directions once we, the Human-YOU, take the initiative to move. The GPS sat nav, like a co-pilot, can guide us through traffic jams and suggest the most efficient route, but it cannot drive the car. We must take the wheel, engage the engine and put the car in motion.

Likewise, if we remain stagnant, rooted in inaction, we cannot reach our destination through our Big-YOU's guidance. We must consistently take steps, constantly adjusting our course based on the guidance we receive, to achieve our goals. Action is the key to progress, the fuel that propels us forward.

Ultimately, the human responsibility lies in embracing action. We must be willing to take the initiative to move beyond the realm of ideas and into the realm of realisation.

In its simplest form, action is the driving force that propels us forward, allowing our dreams to turn into reality.

ON A NEED-TO-KNOW BASIS

Our lives are a complex orchestra, a symphony of action and intention. Within each of us resides a duality, the Human-YOU, the embodiment of actions and experiences in the physical world, and the Big-YOU, the guiding force that shapes our vision and directs our path.

The Human-YOU takes the stage, acting upon the world and performing the tasks at hand. However, it is the Big-YOU who orchestrates the performance, providing the 'How' behind the 'What.' It paints the grand picture, outlining the journey from point A to point B, ensuring a harmonious flow of events.

This collaboration isn't simply a matter of directives and obedience. The Big-YOU is a wise conductor, understanding the delicate balance of timing and information. It knows that premature knowledge, like an ill-timed note, can disrupt the melody of life. Thus, it carefully selects the information it shares, ensuring that each piece of knowledge arrives at the perfect moment, allowing the Human-YOU to fully appreciate and utilise its value.

For the Human-YOU, this means learning patience and trusting in the Big-YOU's grand design, knowing that its wisdom transcends the limitations of immediate understanding.

By cultivating this partnership, you unlock a powerful force within yourself. The Big-YOU provides the vision and strategy, while the Human-YOU executes with focus and determination. This synergy empowers you to navigate life's complexities with greater clarity, purpose and success.

WHAT TO REMEMBER OR WHAT TO FORGET: A DELIBERATE DESIGN

The human experience is a paradox. We are born with a divine spark, the Big-YOU, our connection to the universal source, yet we enter the world with a veil of forgetfulness drawn over our memories. This deliberate amnesia serves a profound purpose. It allows us collectively to fully embrace the adventure of life, unburdened by the knowledge that would spoil the journey.

Imagine a world where we knew the shortest, most efficient route to every destination. Would the thrill of exploration remain? Would the joy of discovery still hold its magic? No. The essence of life, its very beauty, lies in the winding paths, the unexpected twists and turns, the lessons learned along the way. The journey is the adventure, not the destination.

This forgetting, this deliberate amnesia, is not a loss but a gift. It allows us to experience the world with fresh eyes to discover the wonders of existence anew. It also explains why we often have differing memories of shared experiences. Each individual, guided by their own Big-SELF and needs and experiences, remembers the relevant timeline data points that resonate with them, choosing to retain the relevant details while forgetting the irrelevant ones.

This selective memory is not a flaw but a testament to the intricate design of our existence. It allows us to focus on the present, to engage with the world in its entirety, without the burden of constant awareness of our ultimate origin. Through this intentional forgetting and remembering, we truly experience the richness and complexity of being human, a journey that unfolds moment by moment, a tapestry of unique past and future timelines.

THE POWER OF GRATITUDE AND FEEDBACK

Gratitude acts as a powerful catalyst for curating our desires. It works on a fundamental level, mirroring the simple principles we learned as children, saying "Please" and "Thank you". These phrases, ingrained in us from a young age, foster positive interactions and encourage reciprocity.

Similarly, when we promote gratitude for the good things in our lives, we signal to our Big-YOU, or our true self, that we wish to experience more of them. This inner connection, honed through conscious appreciation, acts as a magnet, drawing more of what we cherish into our reality.

Imagine yourself enjoying a truly magnificent experience. Instead of simply basking in the moment, try expressing gratitude to the Big-YOU. Say to yourself, "Thank you, I am deeply enjoying this. Please give me more of this." This simple act of acknowledging and appreciating what you have opens the door for further blessings.

The universe responds to our gratitude, emotions and thus our intentions by mirroring and matching our experience. By expressing thanks for everything, we create a vibration of abundance that attracts more of what we desire. The reverse also occurs that when we don't give gratitude for an experience then then universe will not match and mirror this experience.

However, it is important to note that we can also choose to release experiences that no longer serve us. If something is interesting but not truly desirable, we can simply express to the Big-YOU that we have learned from it and are ready for something new.

Cultivating gratitude is a conscious choice that leads to a life filled with more of what we appreciate. It is a simple yet powerful way to align ourselves with the flow of abundance and development of our dreams.

PRE-DEATH: KNOWING YOUR CHECKOUT POINT

Your checkout point is the juncture in your lifetime when the Big-YOU permanently leaves and breaks the connection to the Human-YOU, and you die.

There are multiple points in one's lifetime when your Human and Big-YOU could decide to check out of the game. The Big-YOU decides these points before entering the game. The actual checkout point occurs depending on how the game pans out and whether the Big-YOU is on course with its life goals and plan.

Near-Death Experiences (NDE) are used by the ethereal realm to reset the Big-YOU back to its task because the Big-YOU became too immersed in the earthly game. Unaware that it was in control of its gameplay, it had let the human do as they pleased, and the human self-had gone off the path. An emergency intervention is curated like an accident or NDE.

The Big-YOU is then given a chance to remember who it is and has the choice, if it wishes, to go back and carry on living. The experience gives it a chance to make an alteration to the human's path and, thus, its life experience or to die and go on to another experience within the ethereal plane or other lifetimes. This creates a new reality and version of your timeline. In addition, both of you are now aware of each other.

What determines the preferred checkout point? This depends upon the level of awareness each has of the other and whether the Big-YOU has achieved most of the goals and experiences that it wanted to achieve:

- Full awareness: The Big-YOU will make an indication to the Human-YOU that it is time to 'exit the game', and the ending will be 'planned' and agreed upon by both of you.
- No Awareness: The Big-YOU won't give any indication to the Human-YOU that it is time to 'exit the game' as it will not be aware that it is playing the earthly game. The Big-YOU, which is still in the ethereal realm, makes the

decision to end the game. This is the reason why essences who 'check out' by this method are confused until they remember who they are.

Alongside the Big-YOU's decision, the Human-YOU also possesses the free will to exit the game through premature death—suicide. While the Big-YOU is aware of this potential outcome, it faces no consequences if it occurs. Rather, suicide becomes a part of the Big-YOU's subsequent life review, providing insights and promoting personal growth.

The sole consequence of suicide for the Big-YOU is the need to reincarnate to explore themes and experiences left incomplete in the curtailed existence. This reincarnation process allows for further exploration and learning.

CONNECTING WITH YOUR INNER COMPASS: EMBRACING THE WISDOM OF YOUR ESSENCE

Connecting with the Big-YOU, which is your essence and your true self, is a journey of deep listening. This listening goes beyond the physical realm, encompassing all your senses—the sight of a sunrise or sunset, the scent of a blooming rose, the taste of a succulent meal, the feel of the wind on your skin, the sound of a gentle stream, the intuitive knowing deep within you and in your heart and the wisdom of your gut instinct.

This inward listening cultivates a dialogue between your Human-YOU, the conscious mind, and your Big-YOU, your essence. However, this dialogue isn't always a peaceful conversation. Like any good mentor, the Big-YOU, employs the carrot and stick method to guide your Human-YOU towards your joint highest potential.

The carrot, a gentle nudge, feels right, smooth and easy. It invites you to embrace adventure and overcome obstacles with joy, happiness, passion and love. The stick, on the other hand, is a harsher, more forceful nudge. We encounter resistance, pain and a feeling of being stuck. It can feel wrong, painful and difficult, filled with roadblocks. If the Human-YOU ignores this guidance, the stick becomes more severe, manifesting as physical pain, shame and fear.

Ideally, the Big-YOU prefers the carrot, guiding you through life with loving support. But humans are stubborn creatures, sometimes deaf to their essence's whispers. In certain situations, such as life-threatening emergencies, the stick may be the only way to snap your Human-YOU out of its complacency.

The key to cultivating this relationship is to create space for listening. Meditation and walks in nature, mindful showers or any activity that slows down the active mind can help you quiet the chatter and reconnect with your senses and thus the Big-YOU. Once you learn to listen, the Big-YOU's guidance will become clear, offering wisdom, direction, and the execution of your desires.

    Embrace this constant dialogue with the Big-YOU, allowing its whispers to become a steady stream of guidance. Make it your practice, and you will find yourself living a life aligned with your true self, a life filled with purpose and meaning.

NUDGES AND THE IMPORTANCE OF ATTENTION

When guidance through our instinct and intuition attempts to steer us in the right direction, it often expresses itself as gentle nudges. These subtle prods may come in various sensory forms, such as a whisper, a thought, a sudden image popping into our minds, a serendipitous encounter or even a physical sensation. They are often a signal that we are heading in the wrong direction or that we are ignoring vital information. However, if we fail to heed these initial cues, the nudges may intensify in their frequency and impact.

Our higher self, the Big-YOU, and spirit guides try to prevent us from straying from our intended path. If we ignore their guidance, we may experience repeated nudges that become increasingly more tangible. This can be in the form of physical ailments, accidents or unfortunate events.

These challenges serve as a reminder to pay attention to the subtle messages we have been receiving. Developing a practice of listening, seeking quiet moments for introspection, meditating and paying attention to our intuitive feelings will open the door to a deeper understanding of these valuable messages.

Therefore, it is crucial to listen to the initial nudges as they arise. Ignoring them leads to more intense and potentially painful consequences. By embracing the guidance we receive, we align ourselves with our true purpose and avoid unnecessary obstacles. Nudges are not meant to be threatening. Rather, they are gentle reminders to stay open and attentive to the path being laid out for us.

FINDING YOUR INNER SANCTUARY: A GUIDE TO MEDITATION

Meditation is a deeply personal journey inward. It is the art of finding your own way to relax, quiet your mind, and connect with your intuition and higher self. The process allows you to open yourself to spiritual guidance, allowing you to listen, absorb, and implement the wisdom that comes from within.

Each person has a unique path to finding their ideal meditation style, which aligns with their preferences and resonates with their inner self.

The type of meditation that resonates with you will feel natural and enjoyable, making its practice a welcome habit. It might involve:

- Retreats: Extended periods of immersive meditation in secluded environments.
- Meditation Practices: Guided exercises, breathing techniques or visualisation techniques designed to quiet the mind.
- Mantra Recitation: Repeating specific words or phrases to focus the mind and connect with the higher consciousness.

However, the path to stillness can also be found in everyday activities. A peaceful walk in nature, a calming bath, driving along a motorway, listening to music or even the rhythmic repetition of cleaning your home can become a meditation, a moment where you listen with all your senses and open yourself to the whispers of your inner voice.

Ultimately, the key is to discover the practices that bring you peace and quieten your mind. Embrace the unique journey that leads you to your inner sanctuary.

RELEASING THE GRIP OF MATERIALISM

Life is a journey packed with experiences, both mundane and extraordinary. The Big-YOU, the core of who we are, yearns for these experiences, for the exploration and growth they offer. While our human self, bound to the physical world, craves both experiences and material possessions, it is essential to understand the intricate interplay between the two.

The Big-YOU recognises the value of material things, particularly when they contribute to a fulfilling human life. However, the Human-YOU can become ensnared in the allure of possessions, accumulating wealth, objects and power, often driven by the fear of scarcity. This fear, rooted in anxieties about lack of money, love, security or joy, fuels a relentless desire for control. The accumulation becomes a futile attempt to fill an internal void, a never-ending cycle of wanting more, leaving both the human and the Big-YOU impoverished.

The experiences we seek are the ones that ignite passion, cultivate growth and connect us with our purpose. They are the memories we cherish, the stories we share and the lessons that shape us. By prioritising experiences over material possessions, we honour ourselves and the Big-YOU to create a life that is truly vibrant and fulfilling.

True liberation lies in recognising the support we receive from a larger force, the Big-YOU, a source of unconditional love and care. This awareness allows us to relinquish the grip of material possessions and embrace a life driven by experiences.

When we prioritise The Big-YOU's desire for exploration and growth, we tap into a source of abundance. The necessary material resources will flow into our lives organically and sometimes in vast quantities, becoming tools to enhance our experiences rather than the sole focus of our existence.

Ultimately, the journey of life is best lived by embracing the richness of experiences while understanding that true fulfilment comes from a deep connection to the Big-YOU, trusting in the inherent abundance of the universe, and letting go of the insatiable desire for material possessions.

BEING TAKEN CARE OF

As stated earlier, the two aspects of trying to live the best life are focusing on what you want with guidance from the Big-YOU and believing that it will occur.

Collaboration with the Big-YOU is very powerful and mutually beneficial because the Big-YOU always has the Human-YOU's best interests. You are its avatar, its access to the earthly game, the immersive connection to all sensory experiences that can be had on earth and the only means for its enhanced growth as a soul in this lifetime. So, it is in the Big-YOU's interest that both of you live your very best lives and that the Human-YOU is happy and enjoying life because if that occurs, the Big-YOU will also experience that.

Also, when it has the life review after it departs the Human-YOU, it will 'relive' how it treated the Human-YOU.

THE ART OF CONSCIOUS CREATION: WHY BEFORE WHAT

We are the architects of our own lives, constantly shaping our reality, moment by moment, year by year. This process, often unconscious, becomes a conscious endeavour as we become aware of our inherent power.

And then what? I like this phrase because it puts the onus of explaining the 'Why' to the Big-YOU on the human self before conscious curation occurs.

This seemingly simple question holds the key to unlocking true empowerment. We must understand the underlying motivation before we manifest and curate our desires. Is our goal driven by a genuine yearning for growth and experience, or are we merely seeking a fleeting satisfaction? Are we pursuing a path that aligns with our core values, or are we chasing an illusion of happiness?

The consequences of unchecked desires can be risky. Obtaining what we want without a clear purpose can lead to a relentless cycle of dissatisfaction and a feeling of a hole or void in our lives that nothing can fill. The human condition often craves more, regardless of what we already possess. This insatiable need can blind us to the true heart of life, hindering our ability to experience the richness of existence.

True satisfaction lies in aligning our desires with the greater force guiding our lives—the Big-YOU, our soul's essence. This Big-YOU, the architect of our being, is the source of our true desires and knows what serves our ultimate well-being. By consciously collaborating with the Big-YOU and presenting our 'Why', we invite it to curate our desires in a way that aligns with our deepest purpose and leads us toward genuine contentment.

Remember, the Big-YOU is not simply a genie granting wishes. It is a wise guide, offering us experiences that nurture our growth and align with our soul's journey. By understanding our 'Why' and seeking alignment with the Big-YOU, we unlock the potential for a life truly lived, a life where every experience and every achievement contributes to the unfolding of our true purpose.

THE WISDOM OF NON-INTERFERENCE: CONNECTING TO UNCONDITIONAL ACTION

NON-INTERFERENCE IS ONE OF THE KEYS TO CURATING THE LIFE YOU DESIRE

Non-interferance

Our essence, the core of our being, whispers profound wisdom. When we align our actions with this inner voice, we discover a fundamental truth—non-interference is the default unless guided by a deep-seated gut instinct. This instinctive call, originating from our essence, often reflects a pre-existing contract between souls. We may be drawn to intervene in another's life because they need to learn a specific lesson, or we ourselves are meant to learn through the experience.

However, our ego or self-worth often interferes with this natural flow. It convinces us we know best and justifies meddling in others' lives without considering the broader consequences. This interference, expressed by vanity and a desire to control, can be detrimental to both. Our well-intentioned actions may inadvertently lead to a more severe repetition of the very lesson the individual was meant to learn.

How do we discern when our intervention is truly instinctive and, therefore, aligned with our essence? It comes without conscious thought, conditions or expectations, a spontaneous act driven by an innate urge. It is the feeling of being compelled to act like a firefighter rushing into a burning building without hesitation.

I watched a heart-warming video of an interaction between a videographer and their dog and a homeless man living on a street corner. Most of us would have walked by without giving the homeless man a second thought. Instinctively, though, the dog bounded towards the man, its tail wagging. A moment of pure joy ensued as they engaged in playful interaction, a symphony of laughter and contentment echoing through the air.

The videographer's heart melted, and instead of averting their gaze like many passersby, the videographer began to visit the homeless man every day. Each encounter was marked by the same infectious happiness shared between man and dog, a beacon of hope amidst adversity.

Gradually, a bond grew between them. The videographer offered assistance, providing resources and support that helped the homeless man take the first steps towards a better life. The dog's unconditional love had kindled a spark within both—a reminder of the transformative power of compassion.

This remarkable encounter serves as a testament to the profound impact of unconditional love and the inherent goodness that connects all beings. It is a poignant reminder that even in the face of adversity, human connection and our furry companions' unwavering affection can provide the catalyst for profound change.

The dog's initiation of this encounter with this specific person seems to have been driven by something beyond the ordinary. It is possible that this chance meeting was a catalyst for a shared learning experience, a lesson destined for both individuals. In this scenario, the dog acted as the facilitator, bringing them together for a purpose that might have been beyond their immediate comprehension.

    Imagine a world where everyone embraced the principles of non-interference and non-judgement unless they have an instinct to act otherwise—a world where individual souls were allowed to navigate their own journeys, learn their own lessons and experience life on their own terms. Such a world would foster a profound sense of freedom, allowing individuals and their essences to fully blossom and grow. Therefore, by listening to our essence, embracing the wisdom of non-interference and acting only when guided by instinct and intuition, we create a more harmonious and compassionate world where each soul can thrive on its own unique path.

ANALOGY OF ROLES AND RESPONSIBILITIES IN LIFE: IN A VIRTUAL REALITY GAME

Imagine you are immersed in a virtual reality game. Your in-game avatar represents the Human-YOU, an autonomous entity within the game world with the ability to make independent decisions and set its own agenda. As the Human-YOU, you possess the freedom to explore and interact with your surroundings as you choose.

On the other hand, outside the game, as the Big-YOU, you wear the virtual reality headset and have a comprehensive view of the game's mechanics and goals. You are responsible for selecting the avatar's attributes, game setting and overall experience, effectively defining the 'How' of the gameplay.

Within the game, various other avatars representing both human and non-human entities interact with the Human-YOU to create challenges and opportunities. These avatars, along with their 'spirit handlers' who control them, and the orchestrated events and scenarios, serve to enhance the player's learning experience.

The essence of the game lies in the seamless collaboration between these three elements:

1. Human-YOU (Doer): Executes actions within the game world.

2. Big-YOU (How): Determines the game's parameters, provides an overview and decides the overall 'How'.

3. Other Avatars (Support): Create challenges, provide support and facilitate the player's growth.

The purpose of the game lies in the collaborative interaction of these three distinct components, ultimately creating an engaging adventure as they all influence one another throughout gameplay.

THE POWER OF BELIEF: A PLACEBO EFFECT

The idea that our beliefs can actively shape our reality, a concept often referred to as 'timeline curation,' may seem fantastical. Yet, evidence for this phenomenon exists even in seemingly mundane scenarios and can be demonstrated through the placebo effect.

To illustrate, imagine that you are experiencing indigestion and heartburn, and you take an over-the-counter antacid tablet that claims to provide relief within five minutes. If you believe in the efficacy of this medication, there is a good chance that your symptoms will improve as expected. This is because your belief has the potential to alter your timeline, replacing the heartburn version with one free from discomfort.

The placebo effect is a documented phenomenon in which a patient's perception of improvement in their condition can be attributed to their belief in the efficacy of the treatment, even when that treatment has no active ingredients or therapeutic properties. Although science has attempted to explain this effect through the concept of a human construct, the underlying mechanism is the connection with spirit and the Big-YOU.

A well-known English proverb states, 'No job is too big or small, only thinking makes it so.' This proverb highlights the role of our thoughts and beliefs in shaping our reality, emphasising that the so-called Big-YOU treats all informational exchanges with the Universal Records, regardless of their significance or impact on our past and future timelines, equally.

Many of the limitations we face are of our own making, originating from our perceptions of what we believe is achievable and what is not. Real empowerment comes from acknowledging and allowing the Big-YOU to carry out its function of doing the 'How' and selecting and curating a timeline brimming with potential outcomes.

By attuning ourselves to the capabilities of the Big-YOU, we can surmount our individual constraints and limitations, thereby accessing the full potential of our lives. This transformation allows us to become proactive creators of our realities, harnessing the power of our beliefs to blend our timelines.

AWAKENING TO SPIRITUAL CONNECTIVITY: NEW ZONE, SAME GAME

The moment of awareness marks a profound shift in our perception. We realise that our individual selves, the Human-YOU, are not isolated entities but interconnected components of a greater whole, the Big-YOU. This awakening ushers us into a new dimension within the ongoing game of earthly existence.

While the game itself remains constant, our perspective changes, allowing us to access a different zone with unique experiences and ways of being. Brimming with potential and possibility, this new environment is a thrilling frontier for both the Big-YOU and the Human-YOU.

It is important to acknowledge that other zones continue to exist within this earthly game, populated by those who haven't yet achieved awareness. These players, experiencing their own unique journeys, are engaging with their respective zones in a way that is appropriate and meaningful for their current stage of learning. Each zone offers valuable lessons and experiences tailored to the needs and aspirations of its players, providing the optimal environment for their growth.

EMOTION REGULATION: MANAGING UNWARRANTED EMOTIONAL RESPONSES

As previously discussed, emotions are the trigger for deeper engagement and exploration of events. However, there may be instances where one may not wish to delve into a particular event by having an emotion. The following outlines a strategy to manage this situation by neutralising unhelpful and unwarranted emotional responses.

The key lies in a two-pronged approach—acknowledging and embracing the emotion and consciously choosing not to explore it:

- First, we must recognise that an emotional response is occurring. This awareness is crucial. We must allow ourselves to feel the emotion in its entirety, from its initial spark to its eventual ebb. This process of acceptance, rather than suppression, helps diffuse the emotion's power.

- Secondly, we engage in a dialogue with our inner selves. We communicate to our internal Big-YOU, the part of us that holds conscious control, that we are not interested in exploring this event. This declaration of disinterest creates a mental space for the emotion to pass by without pulling us in.

Think of it like browsing TV channels. We might encounter programs on subjects we find unappealing, like science fiction, politics or history. While acknowledging their existence, we consciously choose not to watch them. We continue browsing, seeking channels that resonate with our interests.

Similarly, we can navigate our emotional landscape. We can acknowledge the presence of unwanted emotions, feel them without judgment, and then, through conscious choice, direct our attention elsewhere. This empowers us to manage our emotional responses and choose which life experiences and timelines we want to fully engage in.

EMBRACING THE JOURNEY: LETTING GO OF EXPECTATIONS

Once we have a destination in mind, instead of clinging to rigid expectations of how we must reach our goals, we can unlock a richer, more fulfilling path by simply letting go and going with the flow. This surrender allows our inner wisdom, the Big-YOU, to guide us.

When we relinquish control over the 'How' and embrace a spirit of openness, we empower the Big-YOU to reveal unexpected and delightful possibilities. It is like trusting a skilled navigator to chart the course, confident that their knowledge will lead us to our destination in ways we could never have imagined.

This journey, guided by the intuition of the Big-YOU, becomes a collaborative effort. It benefits both the Human-YOU, who experiences the wonder of the unexpected, and the Big-YOU, which finds creative and fulfilling ways to curate our desires.

So, the next time you find yourself grappling with the uncertainty of the path ahead, let go of your expectations and allow the Big-YOU to steer and guide you. Trust the journey and be open to the magic that unfolds.

TAPPING INTO YOUR INNER COMPASS: CONNECTING WITH THE BIG-YOU

CONNECTING WITH THE BIG-YOU

The essence of who we are, the Big-YOU, lies beyond the realm of conscious thought. It is an intuitive, instinctive force that resides within each of us, a guiding light that whispers wisdom beyond the limitations of our rational minds. To connect with this inner wisdom, we must quiet the chatter of our thoughts and turn inward.

Imagine a vast ocean of consciousness, where your thoughts are simply ripples on the surface. To access the depths of your Big-YOU, you must learn to navigate beyond those fleeting waves. You can achieve this by calming the mind through meditation, mindful breathing or any practice that allows you to become present with your senses.

As you cultivate this stillness, you will begin to perceive the subtle whispers of your intuition—that innate knowing voice that speaks through feelings, sensations and a deep sense of inner peace. This is your Big-YOU, guiding you towards your highest potential. It is always there, unwavering in its love and support, offering you the wisdom you need to live a fulfilling and authentic life.

Embrace the silence, listen to your senses and trust the whispers of your intuition. The path to connecting you with your Big-YOU is a journey of self-discovery, a testament to the boundless potential within each of us.

THE BIG-YOU

THE ART OF CURATING YOUR REALITY: 'I REMEMBER WHEN' AS A GATEWAY TO YOUR PREFERRED TIMELINE

THE BIG-YOU IS YOUR REMOTE CONTROL IN YOUR LIFE

Curating Your Reality

The simple act of saying 'I remember when' reveals a profound truth about our relationship with time. It is not just a nostalgic phrase. It is a window into the vast database of our past, a database we curate and access to shape our present and future.

This process unfolds through a fascinating interplay of consciousness—our human mind and the Big-YOU manipulating energy, vibration and frequency—and the universal database of information or, as some call it, the Akashic Records.

When we say, 'I remember when,' we are consciously accessing a specific past event that resonates with our current desired reality. This act of retrieval is like downloading data from the universal database, aligning our present with a chosen past, and ultimately shaping our future. It is a ripple effect up and down the timelines of existence. This is what changed my past, helped me overcome my cough and changed my future timeline.

Crucially, this act of remembering signifies a shift in our present timeline. We are not merely recalling a past event but actively aligning our present with a desired future. This is the key to manifestation and curation—acknowledging that the only true reality is the 'now' and understanding that our perception of the past and future are merely data points we access and manipulate.

The Big-YOU, our higher self, acts as the intermediary between our human consciousness and this universal database. Through this connection, we access and download the desired past and future, shaping our present reality. Our human selves, however, play a vital role. By focusing on our desired destination and timeline, coupled with unwavering belief and an open heart to the potential outcome, we fuel the emotional energy that acts as the 'click' of our 'TV remote', bringing our desired future into manifestation.

This process of aligning our consciousness with the desired outcomes is the essence of all manifestation techniques. Whether it is through visualisation, affirmations or other modalities, the underlying principle remains the same—consciously connecting with our higher selves to access the universal database and curate a reality that aligns with our dreams. Ultimately, the choice of technique is a matter of personal preference, but the core principle remains constant—we have the power to shape our reality through conscious awareness and deliberate action.

THE BIG-YOU

FLIPPING THE SCRIPT: A SCROLL THROUGH TIMELINES

Flipping The Script

    We navigate a world packed with possibilities, each choice leading down a unique path. But what if we could actively shape our experience, selecting the ideal version of events from a vast library of timelines? Imagine a colossal screen displaying countless parallel realities, each a different version of your life, unfolding across time.

    To navigate this vast selection, imagine having a scrolling reel reminiscent of the one in early Apple phones. You can scroll through individual pictures or versions of events, searching for the one that resonates with you. For example, if you desire a sunny day instead of an overcast one while driving, scroll through mental images until you find the desired blue sky and express your preference for this timeline to the Big-YOU.

    You tell 'yourself', 'I prefer the timeline with the blue sky,' acknowledging your openness to the most beneficial outcome.

THE BIG-YOU

The Big-YOU, your subconscious mind, possesses an intimate understanding of all potential timelines in your life. It acts as your personal curator, accessing this vast library of possibilities and selecting the most suitable version for you. While the desired change may not happen instantly, the Big-YOU works diligently behind the scenes, subtly guiding events to align with your chosen timeline.

This is a practice I employ during my drives. Anticipating clear skies and smooth traffic, I find my expectations often translate into reality. While a perfect 100 percent success rate is unlikely, I acknowledge that occasional detours, like unexpected traffic jams, may be curated for a serendipitous reason. Perhaps the delay leads you to a hidden gem of a restaurant, an experience you would not have encountered otherwise.

Ultimately, the Big-YOU strives to orchestrate a life that is not only enjoyable but also rich with unexpected opportunities, allowing you to experience the ideal version of your journey. By embracing this philosophy, you become the architect of your reality, actively influencing the tapestry of your life, one chosen moment at a time.

THE AUTOPILOT OF LIFE: A METAPHOR FOR NAVIGATING YOUR JOURNEY

I greatly appreciate an aeroplane's analogy as a metaphor for life. When a plane is set to autopilot or the Big-YOU, it takes the most efficient route from point A to point B, avoiding turbulence and other environmental challenges. The human pilot, or the Human-YOU, can then use their freed-up mental capacity to focus on other aspects of the flight.

During this automated flight, your conscious mind (the pilot) is freed from the constant worry and decision-making that often consumes it. This newfound mental space allows you to focus on enhancing the quality of your journey.

You can explore new opportunities, indulge in meaningful activities or simply appreciate the scenery along the way. The autopilot will seamlessly adjust to unforeseen circumstances, steering you clear of turbulence and guiding you towards the best possible outcome.

Therefore, I encourage you to embrace the autopilot mentality and trust your inner guidance as you navigate through life. You will unlock the potential for a truly extraordinary journey by doing so.

THE MALLEABLE NATURE OF TRUTH

Truth, in its essence, is a subjective perception shaped by the knowledge we possess at any given moment. It encompasses Focus and Belief—the two human elements of the Lucky Formula explained in Chapter 2.

It can be a personal or a collective truth. It exists as the embodiment of our current understanding of reality, serving as the foundation upon which we make judgments and decisions. Our perception of truth transforms as we gather new information and refine our knowledge.

While consensus may lend an air of stability to certain beliefs, the limitations of human knowledge undermine the notion of absolute truth. Our perception of reality is inevitably constrained by the limits of our own understanding, which can vary vastly among individuals and cultures.

The relentless expansion of human knowledge constantly challenges and reshapes our understanding of the truth. New discoveries and technological advancements unveil layers of previously unknown information, casting doubt upon once-held beliefs. In this continuous process of learning and discovery, truth becomes a shifting marker.

Thus, the pursuit of truth is an ongoing journey of intellectual exploration, critical thinking, and the willingness to embrace new perspectives. By acknowledging the malleable nature of truth, we recognise the limitations of our current understanding and embrace the potential for boundless learning and growth.

Through the relentless exploration of new knowledge and the re-evaluation of our current beliefs, we embark on a path towards a more profound and inclusive understanding of the world around us.

Spiritual awareness and awakening are profound journeys that transcend the physical realm. They invite us to delve deep within ourselves, seeking enlightenment and a deeper connection to the universe.

Just as we explore the world around us through education and experiences, so too should we embark on a quest for spiritual growth. This inward journey requires introspection, contemplation and a willingness to embrace new knowledge and understanding and, thus, our truth.

THE GIFT OF MANY LIVES: A JOURNEY OF GROWTH AND EXPLORATION

Detachment

The notion that 'not everything has to be done in this lifetime' offers a profound sense of liberation and a sense of calm. It allows me, as a human being, to release the pressure of achieving everything I desire within this single existence. This perspective stems from a belief in the interconnectedness of souls and the possibility of multiple lifetimes.

I perceive myself as a vessel for a larger, enduring Big-ME, a soul that has existed and will continue to exist beyond this current incarnation. This Big-ME has chosen this particular human form to explore specific themes, experiences and perspectives. Its purpose is not necessarily tied to achieving a list of accomplishments within this lifetime but to engage in continuous growth and learning.

If the Big-ME achieves its intended goals in this life, that is wonderful. If it doesn't, there is no sense of failure or disappointment. Instead, it simply means other chapters are waiting to be written in other lifetimes, on this planet or elsewhere. This concept of multiple lives fosters a remarkable sense of calm and detachment. It allows me to relinquish the burden of individual achievement, recognising that I am merely a temporary instrument in the grand symphony of existence, playing my part in a much larger narrative.

This understanding has shifted my perspective. I am no longer driven by the urgency to make the most of this life. Instead, I embrace the journey itself as a valuable and evolving experience. This realisation infuses my human self with a deep sense of tranquillity and acceptance. I am not burdened by the need to achieve or accomplish everything in this single life. My role is simply to be the vessel, experience and learn, and contribute to the greater good in whatever ways I can.

MAKING OTHER PEOPLE AWARE OR AWAKENED

Whether you should help someone in their awakening process is a complex question that requires careful consideration. Here are some thoughts to guide you:

First, it is essential to reflect on your situation and whether you feel it is your responsibility and gut instinct to assist the other person. This decision should come from a place of genuine concern and a desire to help, not from a sense of obligation or superiority.

Second, it is also helpful to remember a time when you were not yet awake or aware. Would you have wanted someone to force their beliefs or ideas on you before you were ready? Religions often attempt to do this, and it can be off-putting or even harmful.

Third, it seems that the Big-YOU, or the higher self, is the one that initiates the process of awakening for the Human-YOU. The Big-YOU provides the necessary information and allows the Human-YOU to become informed, ultimately empowering it to start its awakening journey.

If you decide to help someone on their awakened journey, the best advice is to provide information unconditionally and without expectations. This means avoiding any attachment to the outcome and allowing the other person to make their own decisions. Offer resources and support without imposing your beliefs or agendas, allowing the individual to explore and discover their path. Respecting their autonomy and agency is crucial in this process.

THE WASH-UP: A REVIEW OF OUR EARTHLY JOURNEY

Near-death experiences and life regressions often reveal a common thread—a profound review of our life's journey. This 'wash-up,' as some call it, transcends mere introspection. It is a multi-dimensional exploration facilitated by the spiritual realm.

Upon leaving the physical body, our essence can (but not always) undergo a comprehensive review. This is not about judgment or punishment but an opportunity for self-understanding. We see our interactions and experiences from all angles, gaining a holistic perspective that encompasses both our actions and their impact on others.

The Big-YOU, as some refer to our true, core self, embarks on this process with guidance from the spiritual realm. This journey allows us to grow, grasp the intricate web of cause and effect woven by our choices and acknowledge the influence of others on our path.

This understanding paves the way for future decisions. We can choose where and how to continue our evolution, guided by the lessons learned and the desires ignited during the review. Some may yearn for a repeat experience or reincarnate, drawn back to the challenges and joys of a particular 'rollercoaster' and picking a channel to explore a new timeline.

I have witnessed this review process firsthand through regressions, a powerful tool that can offer clients a fresh perspective and clarity on their questions. Through this process, individuals can gain a deeper comprehension of their journey and navigate their future with greater awareness and purpose.

EMBRACE THE JOURNEY: NOT THE END, DEAR ONE

Its the Journey not the end

The human experience explores the concept of time, a journey where the destination is as significant as the path itself.

In a realm devoid of time, desires are instantly accomplished. The joy of anticipation, the struggle of adversity and the emotions that colour every step are absent. The destination, while seemingly attainable, lacks the depth and richness that comes with the journey experience.

This is why the Big-YOU, the essence of who we are, chooses to experience the earthly plane. It is a playground, a stage for growth, a chance to experience the fullness of life—the highs and lows, the triumphs and struggles. Each step, each encounter and each moment of joy and sorrow contributes to the totality of our being.

The Human-YOU is the vessel and the instrument through which the Big-YOU experiences the journey of life. It is the journey, not the end, that makes life a story worth telling.

IT'S NOT ALL ABOUT YOU

The statement 'It's not all about you' is a reminder to consider and respect the people around you. While it is true that, from the perspective of your own consciousness or Big-YOU, your journey and experiences are central, it is also important to recognise that everyone else is the centre of their own universe in the same way.

As human beings, we have unique perspectives, experiences and lessons to learn and share. The Human-YOU serves as a vessel, allowing you to explore and interact with the world around you. By being open and receptive to the experiences and perspectives of others, you can deepen your understanding and enrich your journey.

We, as individuals, are the vessels that hold our unique stories. Our experiences, thoughts and emotions shape our individual reality. This perspective makes it feel like our world revolves around us, and in a way, it does—for us. However, this personal experience is only one piece of the grand puzzle.

The true meaning behind the phrase lies in recognising the equal validity of other people's experiences. Each person carries their own journey, their own trials and triumphs. Just as we learn and grow from our experiences, we can also learn and grow from others' experiences.

This understanding cultivates empathy and respect. It encourages us to be mindful of the impact our actions have on those around us. It compels us to acknowledge the unique perspectives and struggles of others, recognising that their stories are as important and valuable as our own.

Ultimately, the journey is not a solitary one. In essence, 'it's not all about you' is a call to balance self-awareness with empathy, compassion and a deep appreciation for the interconnected nature of our existence. It is a shared experience, a tapestry woven together by countless threads of individual lives. By recognising the interconnectedness of these threads, we open ourselves to a richer, more compassionate understanding of the world around us.

THE GAME OF LIFE: PERSPECTIVES AND GROWTH

Events and situations are neutral and objective occurrences that serve as inputs in the narrative of our lives. They are a collective creation, shaped by all entities and souls participating in this present 'earthly gameplay'.

These inputs, in the form of events and situations, offer learning opportunities and contribute to the growth and development of the Big-YOU.

Our human interpretation, however, shapes our perception of these events. We have the power to label them as positive or negative based on our beliefs, values and emotions.

However, if we approach these experiences with the understanding that the Big-YOU is ultimately working towards our highest good and that this human experience is simply a vehicle for the Big-YOU to learn and grow, we can shift our perspective.

By recognising that the Big-YOU has our best interests at heart, we can view the challenges and obstacles we encounter as learning experiences rather than setbacks. This mindset allows us to expand our understanding and strengthen our resilience. Ultimately, our growth is determined not by the events themselves but by our response to them.

DROPLETS OF WATER IN THE OCEAN

Droplets of Water

The analogy of water droplets within a vast ocean provides a powerful metaphor for understanding the interconnectedness of all existence. Each individual, encompassing their essence, is akin to a droplet, separate yet originating from the same boundless ocean of being that encompasses all life forms, objects and dimensions throughout the universe.

This ocean, a culmination of all individual essences, is the embodiment of a unified consciousness akin to a universal God. We are all facets of this singular, divine essence, experiencing different perspectives and expressions of the same fundamental reality.

To grasp the entirety of our being and fully comprehend this unified consciousness, we embark on a journey of individual experience, each droplet separated and dispersed, experiencing the universe through its unique lens. Despite our seemingly separate forms, we possess the same fundamental essence, power and potential.

Upon entering this earthly realm, we shed the memories of our cosmic origins to immerse ourselves fully in this profound experience. This amnesia allows us to grow and learn at an accelerated pace.

As we navigate the challenges and joys of life, we gradually awaken to our true nature, realising that we are not isolated individuals but interconnected parts of a boundless whole. The Big-YOU encompasses all our experiences—past, present and future—and it is through these experiences that we ultimately return to our source, the ocean of consciousness from which we came.

DON'T JUST THINK, ACT: CONNECTING WITH YOUR TRUE SELF

'Don't think, just act' is a powerful approach when seeking a deeper connection to your authentic self, known as the Big-YOU. This connection initially involves a period of exploration, where you discern the difference between thoughts and genuine intuitive insights.

As you nurture this relationship, you will gradually develop a translation and an understanding of your own inner guidance. You will learn to distinguish between impulses that stem from your human mind and those from the Big-YOU that resonate with your true purpose.

When you sense a genuine connection, it will often feel like an undeniable knowingness deep within you. It may come as a subtle nudge, a vivid image, or a profound feeling of resonance. Trusting this inner wisdom allows you to bypass the mental chatter and take action that aligns with your higher self.

Over time, this practice of acting without overthinking helps you cultivate a deeper understanding of your authentic desires, values and strengths. It empowers you to break through self-imposed limitations and live a life truly compatible with who you are at your core.

THE ESSENCE'S JOURNEY AMIDST EARTHLY DISTRACTIONS

As humans, navigating this earthly realm can prove challenging as external influences and the glamour of distractions constantly bombard us. These distractions are not inherently flawed. They are part of life, offering opportunities for growth and understanding.

The Big-YOUs journey is characterised by its desire to learn and experience. However, the human experience can be complex and overwhelming, creating a potential conflict between the Human and the Big-YOU. This divide can lead to the sense of getting lost or swayed by external factors.

To maintain a harmonious balance, the Big-YOU may attempt to guide us back to the path of mutual benefit through subtle nudges. These can include insights, intuitions or gentle reminders. If these nudges go unnoticed, the Big-YOU may use more assertive methods, such as illnesses or challenges, to gain attention.

Remember that distractions are merely temporary divergences and are an essential part of human life. They are opportunities for exploration and growth. Instead of being bashed around like a fly in the wind and viewing distractions as storylines, we can choose to engage with or ignore them, empowering ourselves to stay focused and aligned with the Big-YOU.

EVOLVING MENTORSHIP IN THE JOURNEY OF SELF-DISCOVERY

As I evolved and gained awareness of the connection between my human self and my higher self, I have come to appreciate the variety of teachers and sources that provide information to me. This information can come in many forms, such as books, videos, podcasts and other media, both new and traditional.

These resources are meant to facilitate the growth and development of both the Human-ME and the Big-ME and to help us discover new things about each other and our backgrounds. This knowledge enhances our experience on the earthly plane.

It is important not to become too fixated on a single source of information, as this can limit your learning and growth. As you and your understanding of learning evolve, your preferences and learning style may change as well.

Therefore, it is essential to remain open and adaptable to new sources of information and to be discerning in your approach to it. If something resonates with you, it is likely meant for you at this point in time. If it does not, it may not be the right time for you to receive this information, or it may not be intended for you at all. Be patient and allow the information to come to you at the appropriate time for your personal growth.

THE POWER OF EMOTIONAL TRIGGERS

The purpose of all events and inputs, regardless of the medium, is to provoke an emotional reaction or encourage further examination of a subject. Your response is entirely dependent on you, the Human-YOU.

Consider the following example. If someone were to declare, "That blue sweater is hideous on you," an individual not wearing a blue sweater would likely experience mild annoyance without any significant emotional distress. This is because the statement holds no personal relevance and may be directed at another person.

Conversely, the response would likely differ if the statement was made to an individual wearing a blue sweater. The words would trigger an emotional reaction because they directly pertain to the individual's personal appearance.

This illustrates that our emotional responses are not automatic. We have the power to choose how we react to external stimuli. Whether we are offended, curious or indifferent depends on our individual perspective and how the information resonates with us.

THE VEIL OF FORGETFULNESS: A NECESSARY CONDITION FOR FREE WILL

The concept of human free will hinges on a crucial element—the absence of absolute knowledge. We exist in a state of purposeful ignorance, cut off from the totality of awareness that the higher self or the Big-YOU may possess. If this veil was lifted and we possessed complete knowledge, our actions would cease to be genuinely free within this earthly game. Instead, they would be the direct result of the Big-YOU's control, rendering our lives predetermined.

This need-to-know principle serves a vital purpose for both our human and higher selves. The veil of forgetfulness allows us to experience the full spectrum of emotions, navigate challenges and forge our own paths, fostering personal growth and soul evolution. By experiencing the world with a limited perspective, we become the architects of our own lives, making choices and shaping our destinies through the lens of our individual experiences.

This delicate balance between ignorance and awareness ensures that our lives are not simply pre-scripted narratives. The interplay between the Big-YOU and the Human-YOU becomes a delicate interplay. The Big-YOU subtly guides us with its vast wisdom, nudging us towards experiences that foster our soul's journey. Meanwhile, empowered by free will, the Human-YOU makes choices and learns from mistakes, ultimately shaping its destiny. This dynamic interaction creates a life rich with meaning and profound personal growth.

THE BIG-YOU

REGULATING THE MIRRORING AND MATCHING MECHANISMS OF THE UNIVERSE

Our perception of the world, be it a tangible object, an abstract idea, or a complex scenario, originates from our 'focus, thoughts and beliefs'. These elements intertwine to create a unique 'truth' for each individual, influencing their emotions and ultimately shaping their experiences.

For example, our feelings about money stem directly from our thoughts and beliefs about its significance. If we associate money with security, freedom and abundance, we may feel positive emotions. Those who view it as a source of stress or corruption and that it is in limited and short supply may experience anxiety or resentment. This emotional response, in turn, shapes our actions and ultimately influences the universe to reflect our truth back to us.

The universe operates on the principle of mirroring and matching, amplifying the energy and emotions we radiate. This means our truths and emotions become self-fulfilling prophecies, attracting more of what we focus on, both positive and negative.

To navigate this mechanism and avoid unwanted amplification, we can do the following:

1. Neutralise our emotions: Become aware of our emotional responses and cultivate a sense of neutrality, preventing the universe from amplifying unwanted feelings.

2. Change our perceived truth: Challenge limiting beliefs and consciously reconstruct our understanding of the world, shifting our focus and attracting different experiences.

Our individual truths are often a blend of external influences—family, society, education, media and culture—and internal perceptions shaped by self-value, worthiness and self-perception. Altering these deeply ingrained beliefs can be challenging and requires dedicated self-reflection and transformation.

However, a simpler path to regulating the universe's mirroring mechanism lies in acknowledging our emotions without judgment. By recognising our emotional state and consciously requesting the universe (through a higher power or our own internal Big-YOU) not to act on them, we can prevent the amplification of unwanted experiences. The universe, in its simplicity, does not require a complex understanding of human intentions, only the clear message of our desires.

Just as a simple smile elicits a reciprocal smile, showcasing the mirroring effect in action, our desires and beliefs become self-fulfilling prophecies. When we focus on wanting something and genuinely believe in its attainment, the universe amplifies that desire, drawing more of it into our lives. Conversely, when we hold onto a scarcity of something while yearning for more, the universe responds by granting us more of what we already possess, that is, the scarcity.

The universe exhibits a mirroring effect that extends beyond material desires. It also reflects our internal state of mind and beliefs. When doubt and uncertainty enter our consciousness, the universe responds accordingly, creating experiences that reinforce those unwanted feelings. This can lead to a perceived 'lucky streak' ending abruptly, leaving us feeling disillusioned.

However, it is essential to recognise that we have support in this process. Through the Big-YOU and the collective energy we emit, we orchestrate our experiences. We can break free from this automatic mirroring by consciously regulating our emotions and acknowledging the truths they conceal.

Instead of allowing emotions to govern our actions, we can become observers. We can acknowledge their presence without projecting them onto the universe. This conscious choice empowers us to direct the flow of energy and create the reality we desire.

We can prevent the universe from amplifying unwanted emotions and beliefs by comprehending and mastering the mirroring mechanism. In turn, we disrupt the cycle of self-sabotage and create a path towards the curation of our true desires and truths.

CAN THE BIG-YOU ULTIMATELY DIE?

The intriguing question arises—can the Big-YOU, an entity representing our broader identity—ultimately cease to exist? Intriguingly, the answer appears to be affirmative. As with the creation of souls, the unmaking of souls is possible.

Crucially, this process must be a deliberate choice made solely by the Big-YOU. No external influence can coerce or induce this decision. The Big-YOU simply declares its desire to dissolve, a transformation back into the fundamental building blocks of existence, energy and matter, contributing to the creation of new entities.

This suggests a cyclical process of existence and dissolution, echoing the concept of reincarnation or the continuous flow of energy within the universe. While this concept is intriguing, it remains a theoretical exploration. It invites further contemplation on the nature of consciousness, the limitations of our understanding of the universe and the potential for self-determination, even on a cosmic scale.

THE ARCHITECTS OF OUR COSMIC PLAY

In our earthly existence, who are the puppeteers of our destiny? The answer lies within us, for we are both the architects and the players of this cosmic play.

Our collective essence, comprising the souls inhabiting both the physical and ethereal realms, collaborates to shape the versions of our game. They communicate and determine the collective focus through a profound connection, guiding our actions towards the highest good.

Residing beyond the constraints of time and space, the architects observe and intervene as needed. They orchestrate changes and encourage evolution, ensuring that our journey aligns with the aspirations of our individual souls and the harmony of the collective.

Everyone is an active participant, and consequently, this iteration of the game continually evolves and adapts. Numerous alternative versions and realities exist, but our collective focus is currently centred on this particular timeline.

AMPLIFYING SUFFERING: THE POWER OF FOCUS AND BELIEF

Our focus, thoughts and beliefs hold immense power, shaping not only our individual experiences but also the collective reality we inhabit. When we fixate on negative events, be it news stories, gossip or personal misfortunes, we inadvertently lock ourselves and potentially others into that outcome and the cycle of suffering.

For example, by focusing and dwelling on negative events or scenarios about your country, such as pessimistic stories or gossip, you are inadvertently drawing these unpleasant outcomes into your life. You may believe these narratives to be true, which can evoke emotions like fear, shame, anxiety or excitement, ultimately triggering the curation of a deteriorating situation in your country.

When you decide to engage with and dwell on a particular event or scenario, you effectively lock it into your current timeline both individually and as a collective. By doing so, you become entangled in the consequences of that negative situation, leading to suffering for both you and those around you. However, it is essential to recognise that this outcome is not inevitable.

We can choose to delve into the negativity, allowing it to consume us, or we can acknowledge its existence, ignore it and choose to shift our attention to something positive. By focusing on stories of resilience, hope and progress, we create a new narrative, one that fosters a brighter future.

The world we experience and the reality we inhabit is a reflection of our collective choices. As individuals and as a collective, we have an immense responsibility to choose wisely. The power to shape your reality lies in your hands, as you can select the world you wish to inhabit and experience.

PLAYING THE EARTHLY GAME WHEN THE HUMAN-YOU KNOWS ABOUT THE SPIRITUAL WORLD

Continuing to play the earthly game when the Human-YOU knows about the spiritual realms can bring up new and awkward obstacles.

It is interesting that when you become aware and awakened, you are intrigued and interested to know more about the spiritual world, and you desire to explore it wholeheartedly to the point where you can occasionally forget about earthly things and do not play the game as immersively as you did earlier. What is the point when you know there is so much more?

But that is not the point of the game—the Human-YOU is not the player of the game. The Big-YOU is. It will oblige and give leeway to provide the Human-YOU with more information about it and where it comes from. However, the Big-YOU does so only up to a point as it had made the choice of coming and playing the earthly game with the Human-YOU as its avatar.

To overcome any potential obstacles, if both of you work and collaborate, together, you can learn and explore the interests of both.

FEAR

As we awaken and become aware of a deeper understanding of our multidimensional nature, we recognise that fear as a negative response becomes superfluous. The Human-YOU is now aware that the Big-YOU is constantly vigilant and protective.

Trusting in this unwavering support eliminates the need for fear. The Big-YOU orchestrates experiences not as threats but as opportunities for growth. Our life map is painstakingly crafted, ensuring that we are never placed in situations beyond our capacity. The Big-YOU can mitigate timelines that are not beneficial to its growth by shifting to a new timeline.

However, the Big-YOU respects our free will. If we choose to avoid distressing experiences, we can make that decision in conjunction with the Big-YOU. The Human-YOU has the power to request an alteration to the script, choosing outcomes that harmonise with the well-being of both selves.

Remember, all emotions are gateways to deeper understanding. By recognising the guiding force that watches over us, we can dissolve fear and embrace the journey with trust and a sense of purpose.

LOST AND FOUND: A PRACTICAL DEMONSTRATION OF THE BIG-YOU COLLABORATION

Recently, I experienced the unexpected loss of my keys. Despite an extensive search, I did not find them. Instead of succumbing to frustration, I decided to engage the Big-YOU concept for assistance.

Applying the 3.5.1 Method, I formulated a clear intent. I asked for the lost keys to be found within 12 hours, either in an obvious location or through an action that would lead me to them. Trusting in the process, I released the concern and continued with my daily routine.

Miraculously, within two hours, while searching for my wallet in my bedroom, I stumbled upon the misplaced keys sitting on a wardrobe. The Big-YOU had guided me to their location without my conscious effort.

This simple incident illustrates the power of the Big-YOU collaboration. By inviting the Big-YOU into the equation, we establish a cooperative partnership that transcends our limited perceptions. It nurtures trust, faith, affection and love between the Human and the Big-YOU.

The Big-YOU serves as a limitless resource, eager to assist us in solving problems and fulfilling our desires. By embracing this concept, we tap into a vast reservoir of wisdom and creativity, empowering us to overcome obstacles and achieve our goals.

OPPORTUNITIES

The universe and your higher self, the Big-YOU, conspire to present the Human-YOU with opportunities that align with your true purpose. These opportunities are not obligations but invitations to choose your path.

By embracing these opportunities, you embark on a journey of exploration and growth. It is a path that leads to the realisation of your desires and the experiences that shape your destiny. While the choice of seizing or declining opportunities is yours, the benefits of embracing them are undeniable. Doing so can lead you to your desired outcome or provide you with exciting experiences and adventures.

If you decline an opportunity, rest assured others will present themselves in the future. However, it is important to acknowledge the opportunity and express gratitude to the Big-YOU. Politely inform it that the timing is not right for you and make a request that the opportunity be presented again at a more suitable time.

The universe, or the Big-YOU, offers numerous opportunities to the Human-YOU as a way of shaping your joint path and helping you exercise your free will. The Big-YOU will continue to offer you chances for growth and development as long as you remain open and receptive to them.

THE TRANSFORMATIVE POWER OF GROUP ENERGY

Group energy is a potent force that influences not only the present moment but also future trajectories and dynamic interactions within a collective. This phenomenon is vividly demonstrated in various realms, including music, comedy and inspirational events.

When a group of individuals with diverse perspectives and intentions gather, their collective energy can undergo a profound transformation. A positive and uplifting meeting, symbolised by optimism and excitement, fosters a sense of well-being among its participants. This positive energy radiates outward, elevating the atmosphere and inspiring heightened vibrations and emotions.

Conversely, a contagious downward spiral can occur when a group is imbued with pessimism and negativity. The sombre mood permeates the collective, resulting in lowered spirits and a diminished sense of well-being.

This interplay of group energy highlights the transformative power that individuals can wield by following their passions and sharing their joy. A single person who exudes enthusiasm and purpose can ignite a spark within others, generating a ripple effect that collectively alters the group's mood and potentially even its future timelines.

By recognising the influence of group energy, individuals can consciously contribute to cultivating positive and empowering environments. Through shared experiences, laughter and inspiration, they can harness the power of collective intention to uplift themselves and others, creating a transformative and harmonious collective experience.

LUCK

The concept of luck often hinges on a powerful belief—the unwavering conviction that desired outcomes will materialise in all aspects of life. This belief becomes a self-fulfilling prophecy. Like a benevolent guide, the Big-YOU presents opportunities, much like offering treats to a pet for performing a desired action. These opportunities nudge us towards certain paths and can even prompt a shift in direction and timelines.

This mechanism serves as a training ground for the Human-YOU, facilitating growth and learning. Recognising the satisfaction derived from successful outcomes, our Higher Self prompts us to repeat actions that lead to positive experiences.

However, it is important to acknowledge that failure, too, functions as a learning mechanism, albeit a less desirable one. This 'stick' steers us in a different direction, prompting re-evaluation and adaptation. While both mechanisms work, the Human-YOU will naturally favour the path of 'luck.'

Both luck and failure function as effective catalysts for personal development. While luck presents opportunities for growth, failure challenges us to explore alternative paths. Ultimately, the Human-YOU gravitates towards the path of least resistance, preferring the seemingly fortuitous experiences that empower it.

The key to unlocking the full potential of luck lies in seizing the opportunities and lessons presented to us. By embracing these moments, we amplify the frequency with which they arise, creating a positive feedback loop that exhibits itself as an abundance of good fortune.

LIFE WITHOUT YOUR BIG-YOU AND BEING AWARE

Do you remember the time when you weren't aware or awakened? Ignorance was bliss. You were ignorant of the fact that you were an integral part of something bigger and that things were happening behind the scenes.

You just lived the life you were served without a consciousness that you can curate your life. You accepted what the game gave you and made the most of it. That is what the Big-YOU wanted, so it is not a bad reflection on your Human-YOU.

Thus, it is not up to the Human-YOU to change that for other people now that you are aware and awake. If they do want to be awakened and they do want to become aware, it will happen naturally on the insistence of their Big-SELVES or guides and spirits like it did with you. They will come across a person, event, information or some kind of media that starts the process of awakening.

It must be natural, spontaneous and cannot be forced. Simply put, the veil of forgetfulness is too strong, and others will not believe you when you force your opinions upon them. They will think you are crazy.

GOING WITH THE FLOW WITHOUT REALISING IT: AMAZING THINGS HAPPEN

When I was a diplomat and went around the world, I used to be what they called a worldwide floater, basically a contractor who went from embassy to embassy filling in for staff members on their holiday or a role vacancy. I did this for 12 years, and in that time, I was fortunate to have lived and worked in over 38 countries.

I am not sharing this to brag but to illustrate the experience of going with the flow. The result will be amazing. What I did not realise at the time, as I was unaware of the Big-ME, was that I was going through life in a state of flow, somebody else, that is, the staff at the main office, was making the decisions of 'How', where and when I would go to a new country to work.

I just sat back and let it happen and went with the flow. And guess what? They were the 12 happiest years of my life. I felt free. I felt completely consumed with my passions and enjoyment of travelling and living in new cultures, meeting new people, enjoying Mother Earth in its finest form and having the best of times.

I had no expectations about when and where I would end up. So go with the flow and see what amazing things will turn up.

TO AVOID UNFORESEEN CONSEQUENCES

When you establish a solid partnership between the Human and the Big-YOU and carefully select the appropriate tools from Chapter 2 to connect with the spirit realm, you can effectively avoid unintended consequences. It is essential to understand the implications of this statement.

Imagine that you have harnessed the power of various techniques, such as mantras, to manifest wealth and become a multimillionaire. While this may be your desired human outcome, an unintended consequence could be that you struggle to cope with your newfound fortune, leading you down a dangerous path of financial disaster, family disruption and eventual homelessness.

The benevolent nature of the Big-YOU allows for such deviations, enabling you both to learn from these experiences. If you become overwhelmed by the wealth and make poor decisions, ultimately losing your fortune, the Big-YOU will allow the learning process to unfold. Once the lesson is learned and the adventure has ended, you will return to the true purpose that you and the Big-YOU envision for this lifetime.

However, it is possible to avoid unintended consequences by collaborating with your Big-YOU and requesting a more measured and responsible approach to wealth creation. By asking for abundance and freedom from financial worries, you and your Big-YOU can work together to select a timeline that ensures wealth is attained gradually, equipping the Human-YOU with the necessary tools to manage your fortune effectively. This way, you can avoid the potential negative consequences of sudden wealth and stay true to the objectives of both you and the Big-YOU.

ANTICIPATION

A close friend recently embarked on a bold decision to leave their long-held job after 15 years. Driven by an unwavering passion for writing and other creative activities, they believed it was time to align their career with their essential purpose in life.

When I inquired if they were apprehensive about transitioning from a secure and structured full-time role to a more uncertain and fluid writing career, they astonished me with their lack of anxiety. The confidence stems from a deep connection to their Big-THEM, an intrinsic aspect of their being that guides them towards fulfilling their true calling.

As they embark on this new path, they are not consumed by fear but filled with a sense of anticipation. They eagerly embrace the unknown, recognising that each step taken is an opportunity to express their creativity and live a life aligned with their essence.

Anticipation, in this context, is not synonymous with anxiety or worry. Rather, it is a positive force that propels them forward. It is the expectation of exciting possibilities and the unwavering belief that the universe will support their journey.

Fear dissipates when we pursue our passions and align ourselves with our true purpose. Instead, we are filled with a sense of purpose and a deep conviction that everything is unfolding as it should. Anticipation becomes an unwavering companion, guiding us through the inevitable challenges and towards the realisation of our dreams.

TIMING AND SYNCHRONICITY IS EVERYTHING

When I was informed by the Big-ME that I needed to transmit this message of becoming aware and how to play the game of life by writing this book, I was apprehensive as I have dyslexia, and writing is not my thing. From becoming awake and aware to publishing this book has taken just over two years.

The reason for taking so long was not only the time taken to get the information from the Big-ME about how the game can be played but also the speed at which I could, as the Human-ME, absorb and assimilate the information.

I had to wait for the outside world to reflect and give me the tools I needed to make it happen for me to be able to publish this book. The tools and knowledge had to come together in synchrony for me to accomplish this task.

I could not have done it earlier because Tik Tok had not emerged as a widespread information transmitter. I did not want to type the book out due to my dyslexia. So, I used a dictation service, which allowed me to convert my spoken words into text through my mobile phone. Artificial intelligence allowed me to proofread and edit the manuscript. Self-publishing needed to emerge and become a thing ordinary people did to get their knowledge out to a wider audience.

So, timing and patience allowed synchronised events to provide me with the right tools and inspiration to complete and publish this book.

DISTINGUISHING BETWEEN THE HUMAN MIND AND THE BIG-YOU THROUGH COMMUNICATION

I discovered a technique for sharing information that helps me differentiate between my mind and the Big-ME. It is to speak without overthinking. While this may seem counterintuitive to the adage 'think before you speak,' children and some adults do this instinctively. The method allows intuitive information to bypass the conscious mind and its filters, preventing second-guessing and self-censorship.

Of course, using good judgment and discernment and employing your mind's filter in certain situations, particularly in interpersonal communications, is essential. However, it is equally important to use your intuition and senses to determine when it is appropriate to share unfiltered thoughts, especially if the information is constructive and helpful.

I recommend keeping a personal journal or recording your thoughts aloud when you are attempting to discern the Big-YOU's communication. This technique has been particularly useful when I work with clients during other-life regression sessions. I encourage clients to express their feelings and thoughts immediately without allowing their conscious minds to filter or analyse the information. This way, they can tap into their subconscious mind's natural communication style.

In summary, speaking freely without overthinking can help you distinguish your own thoughts and feelings from the Big-YOU's guidance. By practicing self-awareness and trusting your intuition, you can cultivate a deeper connection with your subconscious mind and enhance your ability to effectively communicate with yourself and others.

BEING IN CONTROL: A NEW ERA OF CONSCIOUS CHOICE

Being in control

When an individual recognises their spiritual side and becomes aware of their inner self, they enter a new realm of existence, which is the intersection between the Big-YOU and the Human-YOU. This awareness brings about a profound realisation—that the Human-YOU is now empowered and in control of its life and actions like never before.

This newfound power stems from the fact that the Big-YOU has the ability to curate and shape the human's past, present and future by accessing and attracting data from the universal library. This data is used to explore and experience various events and scenarios. As a result, individuals in this state are consciously in control of their experiences and are no longer at the mercy of external circumstances unless they choose to be.

This new level of awareness and control is both liberating and exhilarating. It allows people to tap into their inner power and potential and shape their lives and destinies in previously unimaginable ways. By consciously connecting with their higher self, individuals can break free from the constraints of the physical world and explore new horizons of possibility and potential.

EMBRACING YOUR AUTHENTIC NATURE: BE MORE DOG

What do I mean by this expression? We have working dogs diligently performing tasks, cuddle dogs seeking affection, tracker dogs with keen instincts and guard dogs protecting territory. Just as dogs do, humans come in a wide array of personalities and predispositions.

Some of us are naturally energetic and driven, while others find fulfilment in quiet reflection. Some possess an entrepreneurial spirit, while others value stability and routine. It is crucial to acknowledge that there is no one-size-fits-all blueprint for happiness or success. Instead of comparing ourselves to others, we must embrace who we truly are.

Finding a fulfilling life starts with understanding your nature, unique strengths and what truly brings you joy. It is about aligning your actions with your authentic self. Instead of striving to conform to societal expectations, consider tapping into your inner Big-YOU, the guiding force that knows your true purpose.

What does your Big-YOU want you to do in this life? Perhaps it is to rest and recharge, to create art or to build a family. Trust that your Big-YOU has chosen you, knowing your unique talents and the path that will bring you the greatest fulfilment. Listen to the whispers of your instinct, ask for guidance and be receptive to the signs that reveal your true calling.

Like a dog living according to its inherent nature, live authentically by honouring your unique blend of abilities and desires. Embrace your individual rhythm and chosen path and be the most fulfilled version of yourself that you can be.

EXPRESSING GRATITUDE AND GRACE

When we incarnate into this physical world, we enter into a pact with numerous other souls and spirits to participate in the game of life together and support one another on our journeys. This agreement extends to every person, animal, object and situation we encounter, as we are all here to assist one another in various ways.

With this understanding in mind, it is vital to maintain an attitude of gratitude and grace in all our interactions. Expressing appreciation for the help we receive is essential, as both parties have agreed to collaborate during this lifetime.

The golden rule applies here, 'Treat others as you would like to be treated.' If you perform a kind act or offer a gift, would you not hope to receive thanks and appreciation in return? That expectation is universal in the human experience, so let us remember to always act with grace and gratitude.

BUCKET LISTS: A BLUEPRINT FOR LIFE

Bucket Lists

Bucket lists serve as powerful tools for clarifying and achieving our aspirations. They embody both our focus (the specific goals we aim to accomplish) and belief (the unwavering determination to materialise our dreams). They also include an urgency and emotion we need to complete them with.

By incorporating the 3.5.1 Method, bucket lists provide a structured framework for articulating our ambitions.

The '5' aspect of this framework consists of:

- Destination: The desired outcome or experience we aspire to.
- Timeframe: The deadline we set for ourselves to achieve the goal.
- Criteria: The standards or milestones we establish to measure our progress.
- Why: The profound reason or motivation behind our desire to achieve the goal.

- Action Items: The specific tasks or activities we intend to undertake to reach our destination.

Once our detailed bucket list is crafted, we release it into the ether, trusting that the Universal Force within, our Big-YOU, will orchestrate the necessary means and resources to manifest our intentions.

Moreover, bucket lists represent a collaborative endeavour between our human self and the Big-YOU. Together, we embark upon an exciting adventure, pursuing experiences that bring meaning and joy to our earthly existence. By embracing the power of bucket lists, we empower ourselves to live a life of purpose, fulfilment and unparalleled adventure.

EMBRACE PASSION TO ENHANCE LIFE

Pursuing what you love and are passionate about is crucial because it enables you to focus on taking action for your passion, creating space for the Big-YOU to handle the details. When you are engaged in an activity you love, you may have noticed that time seems to fly, and you are completely absorbed in the task. This is the flow state, in which you are fully engaged and focused on the action rather than getting caught up in the logistics of making it profitable or distributing what you have created.

By allowing the Big-YOU to take care of the details, you open yourself up to the magic of synchronicity and serendipity. This means that the resources, connections and opportunities you need will naturally come to you at the right time. It also allows for the possibility of good luck and unexpected blessings to appear in your life.

However, you may have doubts about whether pursuing your passion can provide a sustainable and successful life for you. It is important to remember that it is not your responsibility to figure out the 'How'. That is the job of the Big-YOU. If you believe that it will not work out, then that is the reality the Big-YOU will create for you. To counteract this, it is important to work in collaboration with the Big-YOU and be honest about your need for reassurance that your passion will provide a sustainable and successful life for both of you. This is part of the 3.5.1 Method outlined in Chapter 2.

In summary, by pursuing your passions and allowing the Big-YOU to handle the details, you can access the power of synchronicity and serendipity to create the life you desire. By working in collaboration with the Big-YOU and being honest about your needs, you can trust that your passion will provide a sustainable and successful life for both of you.

THE POWER OF UNCONDITIONAL GIVING: A CYCLE OF ABUNDANCE

Mutual unconditional giving is the act of giving without expecting anything in return, and it follows the principles of mirroring and matching. When you give, you will receive something equal or better in return. Mutual giving is not limited to material possessions. It also includes giving unconditional love, it can be of your time, of your thoughts, of your actions, it is ultimately being outward looking rather than being solely inward looking and being unconditional i.e. without expecting something in return.

The key to mutual giving lies in its unconditional nature. It is about offering ourselves authentically without a hidden agenda or expectation of reciprocation. This genuine act of giving, operating from a spirit of compassion and empathy, creates a powerful energy that resonates far beyond ourselves, ultimately enriching our lives and those around us.

An outward-looking perspective is characterised by the recognition that resources are not scarce, which allows for generosity, grace, open-heartedness, honesty, authenticity, gratitude and a giving nature towards the world. On the other hand, an inward-looking perspective is marked by selfishness, hoarding, materialism, people-pleasing, self-absorption, isolation, lack of self-love and feelings of unworthiness.

Those who adopt an outward-looking perspective understand there is enough to go around and that sharing resources, time and energy with others can lead to positive outcomes for everyone involved. They are authentic in their actions and words, expressing gratitude and being thankful for what they have while giving back to the world in meaningful ways.

In contrast, those who are inward-looking may focus on their own needs and desires to the exclusion of others' wishes. They may hoard resources and time, prioritising material possessions and seeking to please others in order to gain approval or acceptance. This can lead to a sense of self-absorption and isolation, as well as a lack of self-love and having feelings of unworthiness.

In summary, adopting an outward-looking perspective can lead to a more fulfilling and meaningful life as individuals can connect with others, share resources and have a positive impact on the world. Conversely, an inward-looking perspective can result in feelings of isolation, selfishness and dissatisfaction with one's own life.

A practical application of this concept is the belief that one does not deserve love because they are not attractive enough, lack sufficient wealth or do not possess something they think others may desire. According to the principles of mirroring and matching, the Human-YOU will continue to receive reinforcement of this belief, causing it to become further entrenched. However, when the Human-YOU reaches a tipping point and decides to take action, such as joining a gym, seeking therapy, changing jobs or moving to a new location, this can lead to a shift in belief, causing the Human-YOU to feel deserving of love. As a result, the Big-YOU will mirror this newfound belief and provide the individual with love in the form of a romantic partner or a beloved animal companion.

SCARCITY AND LIMITATION

The perception of scarcity and limitation is a complex illusion woven from both external and internal inputs. On the one hand, it is a construct of the societal game, a tool individuals and systems use to exert control. This societal framework often instils a sense of scarcity, leading us to believe that resources, opportunities and even love are limited.

However, scarcity is also self-imposed. We internalise societal norms, parental expectations, and cultural values, which can shape our beliefs about what is possible. These internal influences, combined with our own thoughts and limitations, create a self-perpetuating cycle of scarcity.

But what if we shift our perspective? What if we embrace the idea of a Big-YOU, a guiding force that orchestrates our lives, providing everything we need at the right time? This belief allows us to transcend the illusion of scarcity and limitation. By trusting in this higher power, we open ourselves to a world of possibilities where opportunities, serendipity and synchronicity become the norm.

Ultimately, breaking free from the illusion of scarcity requires a willingness to let go of control and embrace the flow of life. By trusting in the Big-YOU, we release ourselves from the perceived limitations we have placed upon ourselves and open the door to a life filled with abundance and possibilities.

EMPOWER YOURSELF: THE REFLECTION OF LEADERSHIP

Empower Yourself

In a poignant anecdote from a TikTok video, a newly promoted airline captain faced a moment of self-discovery. As a first officer, he had sought guidance and reassurance from his captain, instinctively turning to his left for support.

Upon becoming captain, however, he experienced a transformative revelation. In moments of uncertainty or challenge, his instinct remained the same. Yet, when he looked to his left, he would see the plane's window with a mirror and a reflection of himself. In that instant, he understood the profound responsibility he now bore.

This analogy holds invaluable lessons for our own lives. Just as the captain realised his self-sufficiency, we must recognise our own capacity for leadership and fulfilment. Turning to the left or embracing self-reflection empowers us to acknowledge our strengths, identify our aspirations and take ownership of our destiny.

The captain's experience teaches us the following:

- Self-reliance is essential: We possess the knowledge, skills and resilience to navigate life's challenges from the knowledge we have gained in life and our Big-YOU's guidance.
- Reflection fosters clarity: By examining our values, goals, and experiences, we gain a deeper understanding of ourselves and our purpose both on a human and a spiritual level.
- We are in control: Our happiness, fulfilment and success ultimately rest on our own shoulders.

Instead of relying on external validation or guidance, let us turn inward to our instinct and embrace the reflection of our potential. By trusting in our ability to lead our lives towards meaning and purpose, we unlock the true power of our own agency. Remember, you've got this, and you are in charge.

Chapter 5
The Trapped Earth—Concluding Thoughts

THE EARTH: A PLAYGROUND FOR THE SOUL

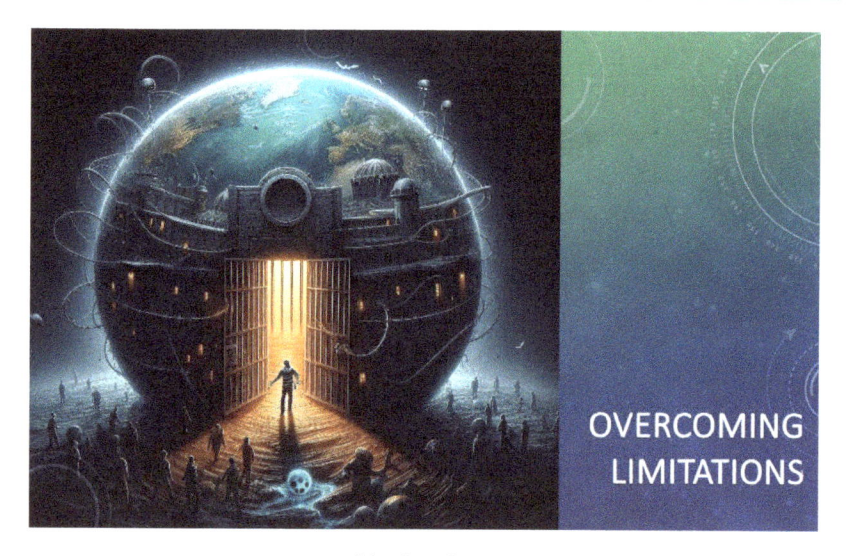

Limitations

The concept of a 'trapped earth' evokes an intriguing perspective on the purpose of the earthly plane. It suggests that Earth serves as a vast, experiential playground for the soul, a 'sandbox' where we can explore the complexities and practicalities of existence without the influences, freedoms and omniscient knowledge of the spiritual realm.

Imagine a child in a sandbox. They build castles, demolish them, experiment with different forms and experience the freedom to create and destroy without consequence. Similarly, Earth allows souls to delve into the myriad emotions, senses, experiences and limitations that come with physical embodiment. Within this earthly sandbox, we encounter the challenges of constraint, the feeling of being trapped and the various levels of entrapment that life can present.

While some may perceive Earth as a prison planet, perpetually trapping souls in a cycle of reincarnation, I believe a broader perspective is necessary. Instead of viewing Earth as a prison, consider it a university for the soul. It is a place designed to teach us about the nature of limitation, the power of choice within those limitations, and the journey from feeling trapped to achieving enlightenment and freedom and overcoming limitations.

The soul, in its essence, is limitless, omnipresent and capable of achieving anything it desires. However, the Earth game provides an opportunity to explore the spectrum of experience within constraints. This allows us to learn valuable lessons about resilience, adaptability and realising our potential. Ultimately, the goal is not to escape the earthly prison but to transcend its limitations and emerge with a deeper awareness and understanding of ourselves and the universe—the growth of the soul.

Fundamentally, the human experience is shaped by limitations. These constraints, both conscious and unconscious, create a sense of being trapped and having our actions and choices confined. The feeling of confinement, while often frustrating, is also the source of much of what makes us human. Through our struggle against these limitations, we discover our potential, forging our identities and shaping our understanding of the world.

LIMITATIONS

Limitations can manifest in countless ways, encompassing every facet of our being.

If you can be aware and identify the limitations you have, you will then be empowered to overcome and dismantle these limitations:

- Physical: Our bodies are the first and most obvious constraint with their limitations and vulnerabilities. Physical disabilities, illness and the very nature of our physical form can restrict our movement, our abilities and our access to the world. Further, our location, whether it is a small town or a bustling city in a developing or developed country, influences our experiences and opportunities.

- Philosophical: The ideologies and belief systems we inherit, whether it is capitalism, communism or any other system of thought, lay down a framework for our understanding of the world and our place within it. These philosophies, often deeply ingrained in our societies, can shape our values, aspirations and perception of justice and fairness.

- Intellectual and Psychological: Our minds, with their potential for brilliance and susceptibility to limitations, are also a source of both freedom and constraint. Learning disabilities, addictions and mental health challenges can severely impact our cognitive abilities and overall well-being. Similarly, mental tendencies like materialism or hoarding can become obsessive, limiting our choices and hindering our growth.

- Environmental: The natural world, with its laws and forces, provides a constant backdrop to our lives. The physical environment, the climate, the laws of physics and the presence of other life forms all exert a powerful influence on our actions and possibilities.

- Social and Economic: Social structures, power dynamics and economic realities shape our experiences and opportunities. Our class, wealth, ethnicity, gender and the people we are born into all influence our social standing, our access to resources and the choices we can make.
- Human-Made: The rules and systems humans have created—political structures, legal codes, workplaces, societal norms—all impose limitations on our freedom. Time itself, an inescapable constraint, dictates our opportunities and shapes our priorities.
- Spiritual and Religious: Our beliefs, values and spiritual practices, whether rooted in religious dogma or personal philosophy, shape our perceptions of the world, our purpose and our sense of belonging. These frameworks can provide comfort and guidance but can also be restrictive, demanding adherence to certain principles and limiting our acceptance of alternative worldviews.
- Cognitive: The way we think, shaped by culture, family, societal norms and our individual belief systems, can limit our perspectives. Our biases, assumptions and limitations in understanding complex issues can lead to narrow thinking and hamper our ability to see the world in its full complexity.
- Emotional: Our emotional states, particularly ingrained patterns like people-pleasing, self-doubt and feelings of unworthiness, can create self-imposed limitations. These emotional constraints can hold us back from pursuing our dreams, expressing ourselves authentically and forging genuine connections with others.

COLLABORATION

While often viewed as obstacles, these limitations can be seen as opportunities for growth and self-discovery. By recognising and acknowledging these constraints, we can begin to understand our limitations and work towards transcending them. The process of pushing against limits, striving for something beyond our perceived boundaries, is perhaps the most defining aspect of the human experience. In this constant striving, this dance between constraint and possibility, we find meaning and define our own unique path in the world.

The Human-YOU, the individual self, can transcend these limitations through a collaborative journey with the Big-YOU, or the universal self.

Critical thinking is essential in this process. By examining situations from different perspectives, the Human-YOU can gain a broader understanding of the underlying forces at play. This understanding can lead to acceptance that these limitations, though seemingly self-imposed, are, in fact, part of a larger game designed for growth and learning. The Human-YOU, acting as a vessel within the earthly realm, allows the Big-YOU to learn and evolve through its experiences.

The concept of being 'trapped' or 'constrained' is not inherently negative or positive. It is merely a state of being, and the Human-YOU's perception shapes its emotional response. For example, cultural or religious norms may appear limiting to one individual, while another may find them comforting and supportive. Ultimately, through this collaboration between the Human-YOU and the Big-YOU, the individual can cultivate a sense of agency and control over their life, shaping it according to their shared aspirations.

By recognising the interconnectedness of the Human-YOU and the Big-YOU, we can embrace the challenges and limitations of life as opportunities for growth with the understanding that they are ultimately part of a grander design. This collaborative journey empowers us to transcend perceived constraints and forge a path toward a more fulfilling and meaningful existence.

AN EXAMPLE OF LIMITATION

Often perceived as a restrictive force that binds us, money can also be transformed into a liberating concept. By transcending societal programming, we can recognise that money, like air or water, is not finite but an abundant resource.

The belief that we are enslaved by financial constraints is an illusion. True power lies in understanding the limitless nature of wealth. The Big-YOU is not separate from us but an extension of our being. It guides us and provides the necessary support for our survival and prosperity.

By accepting our role as collaborators in the journey towards financial freedom, we surrender the burden of responsibility to the Big-YOU. This allows us to focus on exploring and embracing our full potential. In turn, the Big-YOU manifests its abundance in miraculous and unexpected ways, ensuring our well-being and empowering us to thrive.

Therefore, the key to transcending financial limitations lies in recognising the infinite nature of money and entrusting the Big-YOU to guide our path. By embracing this mindset, we break free from limiting beliefs and unlock the boundless possibilities that await us.

My recent day trip to London is a delightful example of how embracing spontaneity can lead to incredible experiences. Arriving in the bustling city, I felt a surge of excitement and the desire to make the most of my time. The idea of catching a particular film I had been eager to watch took root, and I quickly set about finding showtimes.

As I navigated the online cinema listings, I remembered a free ticket I had received through a subscription service. The timing could not have been more perfect, allowing me to enjoy the film and still make it to my flight back to Manchester later that evening.

My day of unexpected delights continued at the airport. I strolled through duty-free, drawn to a perfume I had coveted for months but hesitated due to its hefty price tag. In a moment of impulsive joy, I decided to treat myself, knowing this might be my only chance to own it. To my surprise, the cashier asked if I had a discount card, which I did! The savings were substantial, leaving me with a mere fraction of the original cost.

This adventure taught me the power of letting go and trusting in the flow of life. By embracing the unexpected, I was rewarded with a free film and a significant discount on a cherished item. These moments, though seemingly insignificant, reinforced my belief in the universe's ability to provide abundance.

Of course, life isn't always filled with such serendipitous events. We all face challenges and difficult times. But what this day trip taught me is that we have the power to choose how we experience those moments. By approaching life with a sense of adventure and an open mind, we can unlock opportunities for joy and unexpected blessings.

ALIGNMENT TRANSCENDS LIMITATION

THE WORLD IS YOUR OYSTER

My Purpose

Using the Lucky Formula and the 3.5.1. Method to cultivate a connection and relationship with our Big-SELVES—our true, limitless selves—empowers us to live authentically and embrace our human experiences.

By acknowledging our humanity, we recognise the importance of pursuing activities that align with our passions and achieve our purpose.

When we align with our Big-SELVES, we become receptive to divine guidance. This guidance manifests as insights, intuitions and synchronicities that guide us towards a fulfilling life. By attuning ourselves to these messages, we develop trust in the wisdom of the universe and the belief that we are not alone.

This trust liberates us from limiting beliefs and societal constraints. It allows us to navigate the challenges of life with the knowledge that we have a higher power watching over us. This reassurance enables us to embrace the rollercoaster of emotions and experiences that come with being human and empowers us to lead a truly authentic life for ourselves.

By choosing to live in alignment with our Big-SELVES, we access our greatest potential. We become aware of our unique talents and abilities, and we find the courage to pursue our dreams with passion. This path leads to a life that is rich in meaning, purpose and joy.

Remember, the Big-YOU is always guiding and supporting you. By releasing the constraints of fear and doubt, you can embrace the fullness of your human experience and thrive in the tapestry of life by becoming aware of your greatest and best life.

Enjoy the journey.

Chapter 6
Epilogue: Embracing the Big-ME: A Guide to Living a Conscious Life

The Book of Life

In this book, I have emphasised that we are entering a new zone characterised by awakening and heightened awareness. While we are still engaged in the same earthly journey of life, experienced by both our human selves and the Big-YOU, this marks the beginning of a new chapter focused on increased consciousness and personal growth. The game of life is now approached from a deeper, richer more enlightened perspective.

This life development allows for new topics of learning and encompasses a wide range of fascinating and promising avenues for growth. These topics includes exploring the depths of spirituality and the rich tapestry of human history and its diverse civilizations. To the intriguing possibilities of consciousness expansion, such as mastering astral projection and other techniques for navigating the ethereal realms. To understanding the potential existence of extraterrestrial life and other entities beyond our current understanding.

In addition to these pursuits, I am exploring various modalities that aim to connect with alternate realities and the concept of multiverses. I'm also collaborating with my "higher self" – the Big-ME – to understand how to consciously and fully engage with the earthly experience, maximizing its potential for learning and growth.

Despite the knowledge and understanding I have cultivated, I remain a fully engaged participant in the human experience, encompassing the full spectrum of human emotions. Indeed, this immersion is a core purpose of the Big-Me's incarnation and thus my existence. The remarkable people I encounter throughout my life enrich my journey and contribute to the beauty of my existence. While I face challenges and periods of upheaval, I have come to appreciate the importance of responding to my emotions mindfully. By adopting a calm and compassionate mindset, I choose to approach difficulties with clarity and understanding.

I've let go of fears about external influences and inputs, realising that life is ultimately a collective game—everyone is a participant. I have always possessed the ability to choose which events to participate in and which to allow to slip by. Embracing this insight consciously has granted me a profound sense of peace and empowerment.

I've become increasingly adaptable and receptive to the unforeseen twists of life. While I still grapple with anxiety regarding my future happiness and encounter daily obstacles related to health, finances, relationships, and career choices, I have learned to accept that outcomes may not always align with my human expectations.

Instead of viewing these differences as setbacks, I now appreciate them as valuable chances for personal growth and learning for the Big-ME. I find solace and strength in the unwavering support and guidance of the Big-ME. This presence offers me the strength to carry on with gentle suggestions, and assistance whenever I need it, providing a constant source of comfort and direction throughout my life experiences.

Central to this transformation is the understanding that our **focus shapes our experience** which is a powerful tool for curating the life we desire. By having a clear **destination in mind** and **asking for its fulfilment**, we can harness the power of focus to achieve our goals and shape our reality.

By **mastering our emotions** and embracing the **power of belief through reassurance**, we can actively influence our perceptions and choose our timelines. This includes adapting our environment to support our growth and embracing a mindful approach to the human experience, **recognising that the journey itself**, with all its ups and downs, is the true source of meaning, not just the destination.

This path **has not been without its challenges and learnings**. Disappointment and the need for constant reassurance are natural parts of the human experience. Yet, understanding that **we can switch timelines**, actively curating our own reality and shaping our existence, offers a powerful perspective. We are the **architects of our world**, empowered to access the answers we seek and embrace simpler paths to a more satisfying life.

A deeper connection to ourselves, the "Big-YOU," is **fostered through intentional sensory engagement**. This "Big-YOU" desires a collaborative and loving relationship with the "Human-YOU", seeking to enrich our sensory experience. Trust and a willingness to nurture this bond are paramount. We can approach life as **an instruction manual**, a game with guidelines for optimal play, understanding that **there are no universal answers**. Our individual faith and beliefs shape the reality that we perceive.

Our **voice holds immense power**, a potent tool for inspiring positive change in others. This journey emphasises the importance of **non-interference** and understanding our individual **roles and responsibilities**. Developing **detachment allows for greater clarity and perspective**.

Ultimately, **my purpose is in constant evolution**, as both the Human-ME and the Big-ME continue to learn and grow. This ongoing process allows me to **overcome limitations** and embrace the boundless potential within.

As a result of this heightened awareness of the Big-ME, my approach to life has undergone a profound transformation. I am now driven by an insatiable curiosity, constantly seeking out new experiences and knowledge that will continue to refine my understanding of myself and the world. With each new discovery, my perspective evolves, and I am eager to see where this ongoing journey of self-discovery will lead.

A poignant illustration of the power of this newfound conscious awareness and collaboration with the Big-ME emerged during a challenging family transition when my mother required care due to her dementia, and my father faced a potentially life-saving operation in the hospital.

This ordeal unfolded over the Christmas period, culminating in a heartfelt phone call from my dad, who requested a visit to bid farewell, as there was a strong possibility that he would not survive the surgery. The complexity of the situation was overwhelming, comprised of several critical components:

- My mother needed to be placed in permanent care, necessitating the arrangement of a care package.
- My father was about to undergo a life-altering medical procedure.
- Depending on the outcome of Dad's surgery, we had to decide whether to sell their home or convert it into a flat for his possible return.

- All these arrangements had to be made during the Christmas period.
- We had a tight four-week timeline to prepare any changes required for the 'new' flat.

The task ahead was undeniably formidable. To manage it effectively, I utilised the 3.5.1 methodology along with the "Magic Formula." By working alongside my higher self—my Big-ME—I crafted a strategic plan to address each component smoothly and efficiently. The Big-ME handled the aspects of 'HOW,' bringing forth serendipitous opportunities and connecting me with the right tradespeople. Meanwhile, my responsibility was to take 'ACTION" and engage in the practical human tasks, such as hiring contractors.

The results were incredibly positive:

- My mother was settled into a charming care home, a choice that became permanent just a month later. She seems happy there and now calls it her home.
- This arrangement eased my father's worries about my mother's care, allowing him to concentrate on his surgery, his recovery and to gradually reclaim his life.
- My sister and I decided to transform their house into a flat, which included adding a wet room on the ground floor for easier access.
- We hired a contractor who completed the renovations in just three weeks after Christmas. This work involved installing a new floor, providing a new bed, redecorating the space, upgrading the electrical systems, and reworking the layout to enhance wheelchair accessibility.
- By the end of January, all renovations were finished, and my dad returned to his newly adapted home, ready to embrace his new life.

It is evident that countless scenarios could have unfolded in this situation. By consciously working alongside my Big-ME, I was able to achieve the best possible outcome. This experience illustrates the potential of what can be achieved when you tap into your own higher self, or Big-YOU.

Summing Up

In this book, I've aimed to avoid being overly preachy or dictating how you should live your life. Instead, my goal has been to illuminate the various avenues for connecting with your higher self, the Big-YOU, while also sharing insights on the mechanics of this journey as I've learned from the Big-ME. This guidance is intended to help you navigate the life more effectively.

Ultimately, we are all on our own unique journeys, playing our individual games to the best of our abilities. Your approach will naturally differ from mine. However, I have come to realise that working in harmony with the Big-YOU can lead to the most fulfilling and authentic version of your existence and life path. You have the freedom to engage in this partnership either consciously or unconsciously.

In conclusion, reflecting on my journey of awakening and 'Becoming aware of the Big-YOU'. I have gained valuable insights about the art of living optimally after recognising the concept of the Big-ME. Here are some of the key realisations I've had since this transformative experience:

- **Fake It Until You Make It / Have Faith:** Understand the power of mindset in shaping outcomes.
- **Living as a Human:** Embrace the depth of human experiences, as this is the essence of our existence! The Human aspect of you can now delve into a vast array of ethereal ideas, but remember, this lifetime serves the greater purpose of the Big-YOU. Strive to be the finest vessel for these experiences, allowing them to fully engage with the beauty of the Human Realm in all its splendour.

- **Patience:** Remember that it's the journey, not just the destination, that matters.
- **Disappointment:** Accept that setbacks are part of growth.
- **Constant Reassurance:** Seek reminders of your capabilities and progress from the Big-YOU in an explicit way that you will notice and listen and enact their guidance.
- **Switching Timelines:** Recognise your ability to shift perspectives – we all do this all the time, but now do it consciously.
- **No Universal Answers:** Your faith and beliefs shape your unique reality and thus they are 'true' to you.
- **Agreed Beliefs:** Serve as a pivotal framework through which we interpret our world, influenced by the unique tapestry of our personal experiences and perceptions. Each individual carries beliefs shaped by their upbringing, culture, and encounters, lending a certain validity to their worldview. Nevertheless, there exists a shared repository of knowledge that we collectively embrace, such as fundamental truths about our physical world. For instance, we all comprehend the principles of gravity, most accept the spherical nature of the Earth and planets, and understand that human blood is traditionally red. These shared tenets not only facilitate communication and understanding among individuals but also enable us to navigate our environment with a sense of coherence and common ground.

  Despite the apparent stability of these shared beliefs, it is essential to note that they are not immutable or permanent. Throughout history, our understanding of reality has evolved, often dramatically altering accepted notions. Take, for example, the commonly held belief for the Geocentric model of the universe, where the earth was thought to be the centre and everything revolved around the earth. While in Galileo's time, it was hotly debated (some believed in Copernicus' heliocentric model, others in the geocentric model), some of Galileo's observations (e.g. the phases of Venus) were conclusive enough evidence to falsify the geocentric model. This evolution in understanding exemplifies how collective beliefs can shift with time and increased knowledge, reminding us that what we accept as truth may sometimes require re-evaluation. As our perspectives broaden, so too does the landscape of our agreed beliefs, continually reshaping our fundamental understanding of the world.

- **Your World, Your Life:** You have the power to curate your own reality.
- **Accessing Answers:** Trust in your ability to find insights with the collaboration with the Big-YOU.
- **Life Can Be Easier:** With guidance of the Big-YOU choose consciously simpler paths and timelines when prefered.
- **Using Your Senses:** Engage deeply with the world to connect with the Big-YOU.
- **New Relationship with the Big-YOU:** Foster a loving collaboration between your human-self and the Big-YOU for a more fulfilling experience. Trust and listening are key.
- **Instruction Manual for Life:** Treat life like a game with strategies for optimal engagement.
- **The Power of Your Voice:** Use your voice as a tool to inspire and effect change in others.
- **Non-Interference:** This is a principle that involves respecting the autonomy and self-determination of others, especially in the context of their personal human and spiritual journeys and decisions. This means avoiding the urge to impose one's own beliefs, values, or opinions

on others, and instead allowing them the freedom to make their own choices and learn from their own experiences. However, non-interference does not mean ignoring or neglecting others when they are in need of support or assistance. It simply means approaching such situations with a spirit of humility, respect, and openness, and seeking to understand the other person's perspective and needs before offering help or advice.

- **Roles and Responsibilities:** Acknowledge the different roles you play in life. The Human-YOU does the 'actions' – focus, thoughts, belief and emotions. In contrast, the Big-YOU governs the underlying mechanisms of the 'How'—such as frequency, vibration, and energy manipulation—that shape your experiences. The Human-YOU enacts or actions the how by implementing it into reality.

- **Quiet the external and internal chatter, monologues, inputs and world:** Engaging in practices that resonate with you—whether it's meditation, tidying up your space, taking a leisurely walk, pursuing a hobby, or immersing yourself in a good book—can help create this stillness. By carving out moments of silence, you will invite a profound sense of calm that allows you to fully appreciate the present moment. In this serene state, you become more open and receptive to the subtle guidance of the Big-YOU, helping you discover the answers you seek.

- **Detachment:** Detachment allows us to be open to outcomes that are beyond our current imagination. By letting go of our expectations, we create space for something even better to materialise. We may discover opportunities and possibilities that we never could have envisioned. In essence, detachment is not about apathy or indifference. It's about cultivating a balanced perspective, accepting life's uncertainties, and finding peace in the present moment, while remaining open to the boundless possibilities that life has to offer.

- **Purpose and Themes Evolution:** Witness the evolution of your purpose and themes that you both explore as the Human and Big-YOU expand their understanding. The purpose of the Human-YOU is ultimately to be the optimum vessel for your innate Big-YOU by being your authentic truest self and thus the optimum version of YOU.

- **Overcoming Limitations:** Reassess and transcend the limits you and others set for yourself.

This path toward greater awareness has deeply transformed my approach to life, and I remain eager for the further revelations and insights that lie ahead.

www.ingramcontent.com/pod-product-compliance
Ingram Content Group UK Ltd.
Pitfield, Milton Keynes, MK11 3LW, UK
UKHW052102110225
454949UK00009B/80